TEACHER'S BOOK

THINK
First Certificate

JON NAUNTON AND RICHARD ACKLAM

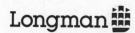

Longman Group UK Limited,
Longman House, Burnt Mill, Harlow,
Essex CM20 2JE, England
and Associated Companies throughout the world.

First published 1989

Set in 9/10pt. Palatino

Printed in UK by W M Clowes

ISBN 0-582-55981-2

CONTENTS

INTRODUCTION

Think First Certificate gives students a thorough preparation for the *Cambridge First Certificate in English* examination while at the same time providing them with a comprehensive general English programme in all four skills: listening, speaking, reading and writing.

As the title suggests, the emphasis of *Think First Certificate* is on students working out things for themselves and developing an independent attitude towards the learning process and passing the exam. The specific requirements of the five papers are introduced in a way which shows students clearly what is expected of them and which encourages them to devise their own strategies for doing the exam tasks.

The book presumes that students will have followed a general English programme to an upper-intermediate level and that they have a good basic vocabulary. Familiar grammar points are checked and revised in a way which allows the students to use their shared knowledge in class, and new grammar points are introduced in a way which makes students think consciously about language rules.

The 15 units of the book are topic-based and, as you will see from the *Coursebook Contents* list on pages viii-ix, the structure and emphasis varies from unit to unit. For example, *Unit 4 Storytelling* concentrates not surprisingly on the narrative composition and written style whereas in *Unit 3 Survival* the exam emphasis is on the Paper 3: Use of English task of completing a dialogue.

This *Teacher's Book* provides unit-by-unit information on how to teach the *Coursebook*. At the beginning of each *Teacher's Book* unit there is a timetable of how a *Coursebook* unit **could** be taught over a period of nine hours in three hour blocks, along with ideas on cutting out certain stages if time is short. Suggestions for homework are given as well as many extra ideas for practice and language development. All answers are keyed and the tapescripts provided.

Think First Certificate and the five exam papers

In this section we will look at each of the papers and how *Think First Certificate* deals with them.

Paper 1: Reading comprehension
Time: 1 hour   Marks: 40/180

The 25 multiple choice questions in **Section A** of this paper deal with the candidate's understanding of lexical relationships. *Think First Certificate* prepares candidates for this part of the exam by:

• looking at the grammatical patterns which a verb can take.

• separating out the differences between words of similar meanings.

• teaching the prepositions which follow verbs and adjectives.

• dealing with the most common phrasal verbs.

Units 1, 6 and 12 provide specific practice for this part of the exam.

Section B of Paper 1 presents three or four short texts which are accompanied by a total of 15 multiple choice questions. *Think First Certificate* prepares candidates for this part of the exam while at the same time developing the learner's reading skills by setting appropriate first reading tasks and by providing discussion points as a final stage to the reading.

To help candidates acquire the skill of answering multiple choice questions gradually, students are given a choice of two answers to the questions about the main reading text in Unit 2, a choice of three in Unit 3 and finally four in Unit 4 where there is a close look at the approach needed to do multiple choice questions.

Most of the reading texts in *Think First Certificate* are 'authentic' and unabridged. Although they are usually longer than those found in the actual examination, they have been chosen for their interest, challenge and the richness of the 'roughly tuned input' they provide.

Paper 2: Composition
Time: 1½ hours   Marks: 40/180

Candidates write two compositions of between 120 and 180 words from a choice of five titles. Question one is usually a letter, two a speech, three a narrative/description essay and four a discussion-type essay. Question five is a composition based on the optional set reading text and this is not dealt with in this course.

Think First Certificate assumes that students are able to write simple sentences and paragraphs but that their ability to write is weaker than their other language skills. Accordingly, composition work receives much attention in the book. Please see the *Coursebook Contents* list on pages viii-ix for how the five questions are dealt with in the units.

A variety of approaches is used to develop writing skills. These include correcting, comparing, developing and replying to 'model' compositions, many of which are authentic specimens of work from foreign students on FCE courses. As a general principle, allow your students to work on writing as a collaborative venture and encourage the process of planning, drafting and redrafting.

Paper 3: Use of English
Time: 2 hours   Marks: 40/180

This paper assesses a candidate's underlying competence in a variety of ways. Broadly speaking, we could say it tests grammar but it does a lot more than that!

Question one is a text with 20 blanks which students have to complete with a single word. This is one of the most demanding parts of exam and also the most difficult to prepare for. As with Paper 1 Section B multiple choice questions, students are gradually introduced to this exam task. In Unit 1 the first letters of the missing words are given, in Unit 2 all the words to complete the text are provided in a box, in Unit 3 10 out of the 20 words are provided, and in Unit 4 there is an in-depth look at this task culminating in a passage where students have to provide the 20 words without assistance.

Question two consists of ten sentences which the candidate has to rephrase without changing the meaning. This is dealt with first in Unit 1 and subsequently in Units 2, 10, 11, 12 and 15. Unit 15 provides 25 of the most common transformation patterns to be found in the exam.

Questions three and **four** test the candidate's productive knowledge of vocabulary within a lexical or grammatical field. There is practice throughout the book for these tasks.

Question five is either a dialogue or completion or a letter to be expanded from notes. Unit 3 provides an in-depth look at dialogue completion and Unit 6 expanding a letter.

Question six tests the candidate's ability to analyse and summarize written information, and the exam tasks can take a variety of forms. Units 2, 5, 9, 12 and 15 have specific practice for this part of the exam.

Paper 4: Listening comprehension

Time: ½ an hour (approx.)   Marks: 20/180

Think First Certificate has a wide variety of listening activities to prepare students thoroughly for the three tasks they have to do in the exam. There are note-taking, *true* or *false* and multiple choice questions for the candidates to do and, as with Paper 1: Reading Section B, the skill of answering multiple choice questions is built up gradually over a number of units. Unit 14 provides a complete Listening comprehension practice exam, the tapescript for which is not provided at the back of the *Coursebook*. All other *Listening* tapescripts are. Many of the Listenings are unscripted or improvized to give greater authenticity and more spontaneity to the material.

Paper 5: Interview

Time: 15 minutes (approx.)   Marks: 40/180

Candidates may do this part of the exam on a one-to-one basis with the examiner or with other examinees in a small group. This is at the discretion of the examining centre and the course director. Marks are given for fluency, accuracy, range of vocabulary and pronunciation.

There is considerable flexibility within the interview but it is usually divided into three parts: one, talking about a photo; two, discussing a short text which has been silently read; three, taking part in a structured communication activity with other examinees or a conversation with the examiner.

Think First Certificate gives the students ample opportunity for speaking throughout the units as well as providing specific practice for these three parts of Paper 5. Unit 10 gives a complete Interview practice paper. Please see the *Contents* list on pages vii-ix under the heading *Speaking* for a full breakdown of how this paper is dealt with in the other units. Also important are the *Pronunciation* activities which are usually linked to a *Listening*.

Please note that you have permission to photocopy for class sets those texts in this book which are followed by the copyright line: © Copyright Longman Group UK Ltd. 1989.

We hope that you and your students enjoy using *Think First Certificate* and that they are successful in the exam.

Jon Naunton and Richard Acklam, June 1989

UNIT 1

English around the world

Possible lesson organization

L1	SPEAKING	Getting to know each other, p.1
	READING	Why English? exs. 1–3, pp.2–4
	*LANGUAGE STUDY	Identifying basic constructions, p.4
	PRONUNCIATION	Using a dictionary ex. 1, p.6
	Homework	
	USE OF ENGLISH	Sentence transformations, p.6
	READING	Why English? ex. 4, p.4

L2	LANGUAGE STUDY	Adverbs of frequency, pp.7–8
	USE OF ENGLISH	Gap-filling, p.8
	*VOCABULARY	Identifying phrasal verbs, p.5
	PRONUNCIATION	Using a dictionary exs. 2–4, p.7
	Homework	
	READING	Paper 1: Reading comprehension, pp.9–10

L3	*WRITING	An informal letter ex.1, p.10
	LISTENING	Travelling to Britain, pp.12–13
	VOCABULARY	The language of airports, p.13
	LANGUAGE STUDY	Question tags and the way you say them, p.14
	Homework	
	WRITING	ex. 2, p.11 (for suggestions regarding the marking of extended writing, see pp.7–8 of this book)

* These are the items that are most easily done by students at home if classroom time is short.

p.1 SPEAKING
Getting to know each other

In order for the class to get a sense of themselves as a group, the following are two possible warm-up activities:

- tell students they have three minutes to learn everyone's name, where they live and, if it is a small class, what they do. At the end of the three minutes go round informally 'testing', i.e. *OK, Juan. What's her name and where does she come from?* If there are still some doubts, give them a little more time.
- cumulative name learning, i.e. each student introduces him or herself and then identifies the preceding students, e.g.

STUDENT A: My name's Ana.
STUDENT B: My name's Ahmed and this is Ana.
STUDENT C: My name's Jean. This is Ana and this is Ahmed.

And so on.
Note You should be the last person to do the activity!

1 Before the actual interview, put students in pairs to quickly expand the questions, and also suggest one or two of their own questions that they might want to add, e.g. Are you married? When everyone has had a chance to do this, go round the class, eliciting the appropriate questions, paying careful attention to and insisting on good grammar and pronunciation (particularly regarding contractions). This should be done at a reasonably brisk pace just to give a firm basis for the interview itself.

Answers
3 Where do you live? (*usually*) **or** Where are you living? (*at the moment*)
4 What do you do (for a living)?
5 What do you do in your free time?
6 Have you ever been abroad?
7 Did you have a holiday last year?
8 How long have you been studying English?
9 Do/Can you speak any other languages?
10 Why are you studying for the First Certificate?
11 What are your problems with English?
12 What are you planning to do/going to do/doing when you finish/have finished the course?

For the interview itself, pair up students who did not previously know each other where possible and give them each a time limit of about five minutes to find out as much about each other as possible, using the questions they have just expanded and others as appropriate. Also, point out they may be asked to report back to the class on what they find out about their partner, so they may wish to take brief notes.

2 After each student has interviewed their partner, get two or three students to summarize in open class (meaning the class working as one large group) what they found out.

Extension
In open class let students ask you as many questions about yourself as they want. You could refuse to answer until each question is acceptable in terms of grammar and pronunciation. If individual students

cannot reformulate their own questions accurately, encourage other students to help.

pp. 2–4 READING
Why English?

1 Give students a short time to look through the exercise individually and then put them in groups of three to check their answers together. As the groups finish, check their answers are correct and ask them to go back and decide on the exact pronunciation, including word stress, of the target vocabulary. The final stage is to elicit the answers with good pronunciation of the target vocabulary.

Answers
1 accent; 2 jargon; 3 slang; 4 pick up; 5 dialects; 6 languages; 7 mother tongue; 8 bilingual

Vocabulary storage
It is very important from the earliest stages that students have an organized system for recording new vocabulary. Clearly, different students will have different systems but you should create awareness of the various possibilities and particularly the range of information necessary to ensure a full and accurate record, e.g. word + pronunciation + definition + example sentence + appropriate collocations. Here is an example.

fascinated /ˈfæsɪneɪtɪd/ = very interested
'He was fascinated by the story.' pp.95-100

For some ideas on this subject, see *Working With Words* (1986), Gairns and Redman, CUP.

2 As it is important for the exam and in general to train students to sometimes read quickly for certain specific information in texts, set a time limit of, say, two minutes, within which students must try and complete this exercise. After the time is up, let students confer and say why they chose the answers they did.

Answers
1 Kurt, Véronique and Adebayo
2 Adebayo
3 Ana
4 Cathy (Rob)
5 Rob and maybe Cathy
6 Véronique doesn't like the way it's taking over in French speaking Canada.
 Adebayo doesn't like English because it's the old colonial language.
 Kurt seems to resent the way that languages adopt English words.

3 Don't set a time limit this time. Let students work alone initially and underline/highlight the parts of the text which support their answers. Then put them in small groups to compare their answers. Where disagreement occurs, encourage justification from the text.

Monitor and encourage all group discussion to be done in English. Finally, in open class, elicit the answers. If groups disagree, let them discuss and justify their ideas across the class. Where necessary, you should act as final arbiter, explaining why a particular answer is right or wrong.

Answers
1 False – *My parents came over about 20 years ago.*
2 True – *Dad speaks much better English than Mum.*
3 False – *I felt really homesick to begin with ...*
4 True – *... had a few problems ...*
5 False – *... one thing I really don't like is the way English expressions have been incorporated into other languages.*
6 False – *We had a real fight ... to keep hold of our French past and identity.*
7 True – *He wants me to ... join his company. I'd rather work in advertising.*
8 True – *If we had chosen a tribal language, it would have caused political problems.*

Extension
Some possible discussion points to consolidate the vocabulary of exercises 1, 2 and 3 are as follows:
- What do you think is the best way to learn a language?
- How important is a good accent?
- Given that there are lots of different 'types' of English, what type do you want to speak and why?
- In years to come do you think English will become more and more widely used? If so, what will happen to other languages?

4 The extension discussion questions above could well lead into students talking about themselves around the points in exercise 4, which would prepare them for having to write this up, probably at home. Where this is done as homework, don't correct mistakes of form, just comment on content, and perhaps make suggestions where students refer to problems they are having. If you are worried about letting mistakes go by, make a note of common errors to come back to at a later date. However, above all, this written work should be a chance for students to really concentrate on communicating their concerns and experiences of learning English.

p.4 LANGUAGE STUDY
Identifying basic constructions

Firstly, be prepared for students to have other terminology, e.g. *progressive = continuous, preterite = past simple, pluperfect = past perfect,* but, at the same time, for the sake of simplicity say that the following terminology will be used in the book and, consequently, also in the class. Secondly, as you go through the answers to this exercise there will almost certainly be questions regarding the appropriate usage of the various forms. Don't get drawn in to trying to give on-the-spot analyses, but reassure students that the different areas will be gone into in depth during the course. Nevertheless, out of interest, it may be worth getting students to indicate via a show of hands which of the various areas they feel most uneasy about.

Answers
A 14; B 10; C 7; D 15; E 1; F 3; G 4; H 11;
I 6; J 9; K 5; L 12; M 2; N 8; O 13

p.5 VOCABULARY
Identifying phrasal verbs

Note
In our view, it is not helpful to make a distinction between phrasal and prepositional verbs or to treat as phrasal verbs those which have a literal meaning. Consequently, a narrow definition of what is a phrasal verb is followed in this course.

1 Put the two model sentences on the blackboard and let students try and analyse the differences. Then ask them to read the explanation in the book to see how it compares with their ideas.
Take exercises 2, 3 and 4 one by one. Give students time to attempt them on their own, then confer and then check answers in open class.

2 Answers

1 No; 2 Yes; 3 No; 4 Yes; 5 Yes; 6 No;
7 Yes; 8 No; 9 No; 10 Yes

3 Answers

1 bring up; 2 put up with; 3 pick up;
4 have run out of; 5 get by

4 Answers

1 get by; 2 picked up; 3 ran out of; 4 put up with;
5 have brought up

p.6 USE OF ENGLISH
Sentence transformations

As this kind of exercise may be new for some or all of the students, it will probably be wise to work through the first few as a class together. Emphasize that the second sentence must have the same meaning as the first and that where possible the words from the first sentence should be re-used in the second.

Answers
1 I'm bilingual because/as we still speak Italian at home. (*See Rob Giuliani text*)
2 Dad speaks (much) better English than Mum./Dad speaks English better than Mum. (*See Rob Giuliani text*)
3 Her accent is so strong that some people can't understand her. (*See Rob Giuliani text*)
4 I have been studying business administration in London for the past two years. (*See Cathy Wong text*)

5 I was sent to an English-speaking school (by my parents). (*See Cathy Wong text*)
6 It is useful to know English. (*See Kurt Thommen text*)
7 He doesn't speak slowly enough for me to understand. (*See Kurt Thommen text*)
8 My biggest problem is pronunciation. (*See Ana Gonzales text*)
9 It is eight years since I started to learn English. (*See Ana Gonzales text*)
10 If we had chosen a tribal language, it would have caused political problems/we would have had political problems. (*See Adebayo Omere text*)

pp. 6–7 PRONUNCIATION
Using a dictionary

Open this section with an informal class discussion along the following lines:

• How many of you have dictionaries?
• What kinds of dictionaries are they?

Ask students to comment on dictionaries they have used and any particular good or bad features they have noticed. Brainstorm all the different information a good dictionary can provide, including pronunciation. Point out the need to understand phonemics to be able to make use of this facility.

Note
As there are frequent opportunities provided by this course for students to consult dictionaries, it is worth recommending that students have their own dictionary which they bring to class. Alternatively, there should always be one or two dictionaries available in the classroom.

1 The sounds (*phonemes*) of English

Make sure students are able to pronounce the various phonemes correctly before they attempt to think of other example words containing the target sounds. Put students in groups to come up with other examples. At the end, elicit from the groups as many different real words as possible to exemplify each sound. You may find that students have chosen words with very similar spelling to the original, in which case you may want to put the following words on the blackboard and ask students to allocate them to the appropriate phoneme: said, this, book, think ,meat, heart, done, tomorrow, win, heard, hat, do, gone.
   This should serve to emphasize the lack of relationship there is between the spelling of a word and its pronunciation in English, reinforcing the need for students to keep a record of the pronunciation of new items of vocabulary.
   You may feel that for your class to go over all the phonemes in one lesson is too much, in which case this can be broken down into, e.g. vowels, diphthongs, consonants, and a small slot done on each over subsequent lessons.

2 Word stress

You might like to give the example of *important*. If the stress is wrongly placed on the first syllable this becomes *impotent*, a fairly significant change in meaning!

Working in small groups, any or all of exercises 2, 3 and 4 could be done competitively to see which team can finish first. Whether or not you set up exercises in the form of a 'competition' will depend on
a) how *your class* will react and b) how *you* feel about it.

Answers

1 /æd'vɜ:tɪzmənt/   11 /kəmju:nɪ'keɪʃən/
2 /'ædvətaɪzɪŋ/   12 /prə'naʊns/
3 /ɪn'dʌstrɪəl/   13 /prənʌnsɪ'eɪʃən/
4 /'ɪndəstrɪ/
5 /'ægrɪkʌltʃə/
6 /'fəʊtəgra:f/
7 /fə'tɒgrəfɪ/
8 /fəʊtə'græfɪk/
9 /fə'tɒgrəfə/
10 /kə'mju:nɪkeɪt/

3 Answers

1 first; 2 certificate; 3 examination; 4 question;
5 answer; 6 language; 7 dictionary; 8 official;
9 afterwards; 10 chocolate; 11 usually; 12 English;
13 important; 14 think; 15 peas

Extension

For a little fun, after exercise 4, students may like to try saying these sentences:
• Pronunciation is very important for successful communication.
• The first advertisement was for an industrial photographer.
• Peas were never his favourite vegetable.
• Afterwards, he started to argue with the air hostess when she asked him to move his baggage out of the aisle.
• If he's not in the comfortable chair, he usually starts to cough.

4

Please refer to a dictionary for the answers.

pp. 7–8 LANGUAGE STUDY
Adverbs of frequency

1 Answers

<u><never rarely/seldom occasionally sometimes often usually always></u>

2 Answers

1 Wrong – *She seldom uses ...*
2 Right – but it is more common to say *We occasionally read ...*
3 Right
4 Wrong – *She always comes to class late ...*
5 Wrong – *He is sometimes late.*
6 Wrong – *He never checks ...*
7 Wrong – *He often gives ...*
8 Right
9 Wrong – *We usually study ...*
10 Wrong – *They always go ...*
11 Wrong – *Do you often speak ...*
12 Right
13 Wrong – *We should always ...*
14 Right

3 Answers

1/2 The safest place to put these adverbs is **after** the verb *be* but **before** all other verbs.
3 The adverb is put **after** modals like *can, will* and *should.*

After exercise 3, see if students have any other adverbs of frequency they want to add to the list. Students may bring up expressions of definite frequency, e.g.

once
twice | *a day/week/month/year*
three times

4

Either do this in pairs and then report back in open class or divide the class into groups with each group taking one question and conducting a mini-class survey covering all the students. (To organize a class survey, get students to stand up and move around the classroom, asking as many other students as possible their question/s.) Make sure students are aware of the question form *How often do you ...?* At the end get students to report back along the lines of *15 people in the class rarely speak English outside the class, but only two people never speak English outside.*

Extension

a) A discussion of *How often is often?* in relation to different activities, e.g. eating out, having a row with your parents, and so on. Ideas of what *occasionally/ sometimes/often* mean can vary dramatically.
b) This could possibly lead in to discussing the different *realistic* opportunities that exist for contact with English outside the classroom, with students contributing what they already do. Outside of an English-speaking environment some examples might be: listening to the BBC World Service, going to films in English, reading English books/magazines/papers and making penfriends. It needs to be stressed that in order to do well in the exam the more exposure outside the classroom to English, the better. Clearly there is not time for students to do everything but they should choose at least one area they are interested in,

e.g. current affairs and, in this case, make an effort to *regularly* read a paper in English, e.g. once a week.

p.8 USE OF ENGLISH

Put students in small groups and get them together to estimate the answers to the following questions:

- How many people now speak English as their mother tongue? (*over 300 million*)
- How many people use it as a foreign language? (*another billion*)
- What fraction of the world's mail is in English? (¾)
- What fraction of all scientists write in English? (⅔)

Having done this, students compare their ideas in open class and then quickly scan the text for the answers. Then ask students to read through the text again, this time to decide in a few words the **basic topic** of each paragraph, i.e. Paragraph 1: the growth in the use of English. Paragraph 2: English as an official language. Paragraph 3: the increasing desire to learn English. Paragraph 4: motivating factors to learn English. Finally, let them work together to complete the gaps.

Answers
1 suggest; 2 widespread; 3 minority; 4 official; 5 belonging; 6 published; 7 Nowadays; 8 elementary; 9 pharmacy; 10 tourism; 11 written; 12 computers; 13 negotiate; 14 negotiations; 15 studying

pp.9–10 READING
Paper 1: Reading comprehension

1 Ask students to quickly try and do each question, covering what is beneath. They should discuss together the questions before uncovering the answers/explanations. Encourage students to add new vocabulary and collocations to their vocabulary records.

Answers
1 B; 2 C; 3 C; 4 A; 5 D; 6 B; 7 B; 8 B; 9 C; 10 B; 11 A; 12 A

pp.10–11 WRITING
An informal letter

Many students have particular problems with the layout of informal letters and you may wish to make students conscious of the peculiarities in the construction of informal letters in English. In this case, begin by asking the following questions:

When you are sending an informal letter:
- where do you put your name and address/the date/ the address of the person you are writing to?
- how do you begin the letter?
- where do you generally begin the first and subsequent paragraphs?
- what expressions might you use to finish the letter?

- what do you put if you want to add something after your signature that you forgot to put in the main part of the letter?

Having thought about this, let students look at the letter to check their ideas.

1 Students then read the letter to answer the various comprehension questions.

Point out the need for clear paragraphing with one basic topic contained within each paragraph.

Answers
1 They'll meet outside customs and immigration on 25th October.
2 She advises her to bring a warm coat and strong boots, and also a camera.
3 She wants to be an interpreter, or to work for an international company.
4 In the same room as Caroline.
5 For Marisol to bring some cigarettes for her father.

A final stage might be for students to go through the letter and underline any general expressions that they feel could be useful when they come to write similar informal letters themselves. Set exercise 2 as homework.

pp.12–13 LISTENING
Travelling to Britain

After each listening, let students confer. If students find it relatively straightforward, go over the answers immediately. Otherwise remind/tell them that in the exam they will hear all listening texts twice and play them again. If there is still disagreement about the correct answer, play the specific part which contains the answer. If necessary, elicit word by word until the answer is clear to all.

1 Checking in

Tapescript
GROUND STEWARD: Afternoon, madam. Could I have your ticket, please? Thank you. Would you like smoking or non-smoking?
MARISOL: Non-smoking. I would like a window seat too.
GROUND STEWARD: Let me see now. No, I'm sorry. We've got no seats left in the non-smoking area. We've got some left in the smoking area.
MARISOL: No, no, no. I wanted non-smoking please.
GROUND STEWARD: I see. Yes, I've got one. It's an aisle seat. Is that all right?
MARISOL: An aisle seat? What's an *aisle* seat? Sorry.
GROUND STEWARD: It's on the end of the row of seats – it's where the people walk up and down. You know?
MARISOL: Oh yes. Yes, that's OK.
GROUND STEWARD: Oh, right. OK, then I can give you Seat P3. Would you put your luggage on the scales please? I'm awfully sorry, madam you're two kilos over.

MARISOL: Two kilos! But I thought you were allowed 22 kilos. I weighed my luggage before I left home and I had 22 kilos.

GROUND STEWARD: No, I'm sorry, Madam. It's ... the limit is 20 kilos. But look, why don't you take something out of your baggage and put in your hand luggage? And then you'll be OK.

MARISOL: Oh! OK, thank you very much.

GROUND STEWARD: Oh, no problem. Let's see. Now here's your boarding card and your ticket.

MARISOL: Thank you.

GROUND STEWARD: Bye bye.

MARISOL: Bye bye.

Answers
1 False – *she has an aisle seat.*
2 True.
3 False – *it is P3.*
4 True
5 True.

2 The captain's announcement

Tapescript

CAPTAIN: Good afternoon, ladies and gentlemen. This is Captain Anderson speaking. On behalf of myself and the crew, I'd like to welcome you on board this Air Magnesia flight to London. May I apologize for the short delay in our departure. This was caused by a problem with one of our tyres but everything's all right now and we should be able to make up for the lost time. We shall be flying at an altitude of 30,000 feet and our estimated time of arrival is 19.30 local time. Weather conditions are good but we may experience a little turbulence for the first 30 minutes so I would suggest you keep your safety belts fastened. During the flight, dinner will be served and our cabin crew will be ...

Answers
1 problems with one of the tyres
2 19.30 hours, local time.
3 30,000 feet

3 Buying duty-free

Tapescript

STEWARDESS: Duty free?

MARISOL: Yes, please. What sort of perfume do you have?

STEWARDESS: We've got three kinds: Blue Lady, Jennifer and Seduction. Is it for you?

MARISOL: No, it's for a lady of about 50.

STEWARDESS: Well, Jennifer might be a bit young then.

MARISOL: I see. What's the difference between the other two?

STEWARDESS: Well, Seduction's quite a bit more expensive.

MARISOL: Can you tell me how much they cost?

STEWARDESS: Seduction starts at £9 for a small bottle. For the same price you could have a medium sized bottle of Blue Lady.

MARISOL: I'll take the Blue Lady at £9.

STEWARDESS: Anything else?

MARISOL: Yes, could I have two hundred Winchester, please?

STEWARDESS: I'm afraid we've just run out.

MARISOL: Oh, in that case, I'll have a carton of Churchill's.

STEWARDESS: Here you are. Is that all?

MARISOL: Yeah.

STEWARDESS: Now, that'll be £18.50.

MARISOL: Can I pay in pesetas, please?

STEWARDESS: Yes, that'll be fine.

Answers
Perfume: *Blue Lady – medium size*
Cigarettes: *Churchill*

4 The lost luggage

Tapescript

OFFICIAL: So you've arrived from Spain and you've lost your luggage.

MARISOL: Yes, that's right. I've lost all my things.

OFFICIAL: Now, don't you worry. Bags usually turn up quite quickly, you know. You kept your receipts, didn't you?

MARISOL: Yes, of course.

OFFICIAL: Good. Right then, could you describe the bags to me, please?

MARISOL: Yes, there is a suitcase and a holdall.

OFFICIAL: What's the suitcase like?

MARISOL: It's red and it's got a brown leather strap around.

OFFICIAL: Bright red?

MARISOL: No, dark.

OFFICIAL: Anything else you could say to describe it?

MARISOL: It's quite large.

OFFICIAL: I see.

MARISOL: And it's got the address of where I am staying in England on the label.

OFFICAL: Good. And the holdall? Is it a bag or a case?

MARISOL: A bag. And it's dark blue with red handles.

OFFICIAL: Fine.

MARISOL: Again, it's quite big. The sort of thing tennis players use. Do you know what I mean?

OFFICIAL: Yes.

MARISOL: You will find them, won't you?

OFFICIAL: I'm sure we will. OK, if you'd just like to wait over there for a few minutes. I'll go and have a look to see if your stuff is on the trolley. Keep your fingers crossed.

Answers

p.13 VOCABULARY
The language of airports

Having done the listening exercises, put students in pairs and together let them re-tell what happened to Marisol. Perhaps, at the end, pick out one good student to do it in front of the class. Then tell them to read the text with gaps (*The language of airports*) and see if there is any additional information in the text. Then read through again and complete.

Answers
1 charter; 2 scheduled; 3 check-in;
4 boarding card; 5 excess baggage; 6 aisle;
7 departure lounge; 8 gate; 9 passengers;
10 crew; 11 took off; 12 runway; 13 stewardess;
14 duty-free; 15 landed; 16 baggage claim;
17 customs; 18 immigration

Students who finish early should check their answers with other early finishers and then together decide on the correct stress and pronunciation of the gapped words. Final feedback – read the text aloud around the class focusing on good pronunciation. If serious problems arise with any target vocabulary, analyse them by asking students to identify stress position, appropriate phonemes and so on.

Extension
Ask students if any of them have had any unpleasant flying experiences – if there are a few, then put students into groups to listen to one each. If there are only one or two, do this in open class. If there are none, then you may want to tell your own if you have one. As further consolidation, students could be asked to write up the *bad flying experience* account they listened to.

p.14 LANGUAGE STUDY
Question tags and the way you say them

1 Before referring to the book, play the relevant extracts from Listening exercise 4: *You kept the receipts, didn't you?* and *You will find them, won't you?* Ask if in the first extract the airport official is checking something he is fairly sure about (Yes) and if in the second extract Marisol is fairly sure they will find them (No). Elicit from students how they know the answers, i.e. from the intonation. Get students to describe the intonation patterns. Read through this section.

2 Tapescript and Answers
1 You're married, aren't you? (*real question*)
2 It's cold, isn't it? (*checking*)
3 You'll have some cake, won't you? (*real*)
4 You'd like to go, wouldn't you? (*checking*)
5 She's got three brothers, hasn't she? (*checking*)

3 Answers
1 isn't it? 2 don't we? 3 didn't she? 4 haven't you?
5 hadn't we? 6 doesn't she? 7 won't you?* 8 aren't I?
9 shall we?* 10 does he?
* These are exceptions to the rule:

Extension
As freer practice, students could be asked to act out the scene between Marisol and the airport official.

Notes on marking written homework

In order for students to be adequately prepared for the exam and, in particular, Paper 2, they need to be given regular written homework, both controlled, e.g. cloze texts, sentence transformation exercises and other grammatical exercises, and less controlled, e.g. various types of composition.

In order to develop the self-critical awareness of students towards their own work, various techniques can be employed in relation to the freer written work. Where compositions are set and students are being marked on all aspects of their English, a marking code should be adopted which will direct students towards the type of mistake they have been making. They can then correct the mistake themselves or work on it in pairs or small groups. On the next page is an example based on the writing task on Coursebook p.11.

I have 19 years old. I live at the middle of
Paris. I am ∧ student at the Sorbonne and
I study english at a language school in the
evenings. I studied english since 6 years. I
enjoy to play squash, tenis and rugby but
I have always to make my homework in the
evenings wich mean I don't have a lot
of free time.

(WW) = wrong word
(WO) = word order
(SP) = spelling
(P) = punctuation
(t) = tense
(gr) = grammar
∧ = word missing
? = meaning not clear
// = new paragraph
TA = try this section again

It is important, however, to use such a code only in cases where you believe students will be able to self-correct. During the course, you may want to progressively give less and less direct indication of where mistakes are and of what type as clearly in the exam itself students will have no such help. An interim stage can be to put a number at the beginning of each line indicating how many mistakes have been made.

To reduce the time spent on correcting homework in class, it can be useful to prepare a list of ten or so sentences from students' work that incorporate typical mistakes for students to work on together. This can be instructive for all and cut down the amount each individual has to correct in their own work.

If there has been some preparatory work in class on a particular area, e.g. narrative tenses (*see Unit 4*), and students are subsequently set a narrative composition for homework, it is important that, in marking the homework, you particularly focus on the target language area – either to praise the successful application of target language in context or to give directions for correction.

So that the marking of students' written work does not become too negative a process, when a particularly good piece of written work is produced, photocopy it and give copies to all the students in the class in order that they can analyse what has made this so good.

After students have become accustomed to critically analysing their own work, you may want to ask students to spend time considering each other's work in small groups **before** they hand it in to be marked. In these groups they can try and detect mistakes and think of better ways of expressing what is intended.

As the exam approaches, it is important that students are told/shown the criteria by which their compositions are going to be marked. Having explained the system, start marking their work with explicit reference to the relevant criteria.

18–20	Excellent	Natural English with minimal errors and complete realization of the task set.
16–17	Very Good	Good vocabulary and structure, above the simple sentence level. Errors non-basic.
12–15	Good	Simple but accurate realization of task. Sufficient naturalness, not many errors.
8–11	Pass	Reasonably correct if awkward OR natural treatment of subject with some serious errors.
5–7	Weak	Vocabulary and grammar inadequate for the task set.
0–4	Very Poor	Incoherent. Errors showing lack of basic knowledge of English.

Right from the beginning of the course students should keep their own *Personal Mistakes Record Sheet*. They should make a note on this of all mistakes they make which they have a tendency to repeat, divided into appropriate categories, e.g.

SPELLING
wich ✗   which ✓

GRAMMAR
since 10 years ✗   for 10 years ✓

PUNCTUATION
august ✗   August ✓

This record sheet should be used as a checklist prior to the handing in of written work and also should be mentally gone through before students give in their compositions in the final exam.

UNIT 2

Time out

Possible lesson organization

L1		
	SPEAKING	Entertainment questionnaire, p.15
	LISTENING	An evening at the cinema, p.16
	LANGUAGE STUDY	It's time/I'd rather + Short replies, pp.16–17
	SPEAKING	An evening out, p.17
	WRITING	An informal letter exs. 1–4 (except part 3 of ex. 4), pp. 24–25
	Homework	
	WRITING	ex. 4 part 3, p.25

L2		
	READING	Fiction to capture the imagination, pp.18–19
	*USE OF ENGLISH	p.19
	LANGUAGE STUDY	Past simple or present perfect? + When we use the present perfect exs. 1–4, pp.20–21
	PRONUNCIATION	Sentence stress, p.21
	SPEAKING	Role play, p.21
	Homework	
	Write a newspaper article based on the role play.	

L3		
	READING	Star quality, pp. 22–23
	*USE OF ENGLISH	Changing verbs to nouns, p.23
	VOCABULARY	Phrasal verbs with **take**, p.24
	USE OF ENGLISH	exs. 1 – 3 (up to planning the speech), p.26
	USE OF ENGLISH	The Smith Family, pp.26–27
	Homework	
	USE OF ENGLISH	Sentence Transformation , p.25
	USE OF ENGLISH	ex. 3 (writing the speech), p.26

These are the items that are most easily done by students at home if classroom time is short.

p.15 SPEAKING

Either do a quick two minute brainstorm of different types of entertainment **or** put up anagrams of types of entertainment on the blackboard, e.g. XGNBIO (*boxing*), RAPEO (*opera*) and so on for students to work out. Then go round the class eliciting students' opinions

about the different forms of entertainment, e.g. *How do you feel about boxing?* Attempt to elicit the various response types in the Coursebook, feeding in the language where appropriate. Students complete the questionnaire and compare with a partner.

Extension
You might wish to give prompts to encourage more discussion, e.g. *Why do you enjoy these particular activities? How long have you been doing them? How did you first come to start doing them? Are there any free-time activities you would like to do but have never got round to?*

p.16 LISTENING

1 What's on at the cinema

In small groups get students to talk about any good films they have seen recently, where they are on and so on. Possibly link this to talking about what types of films different students are *keen on.*

As usual, give students time to look at the task first. Let them listen once, confer and then listen again to check. If any disagreements remain, play the specific part of the tape so students can focus on the correct answer.

Tapescript
RECORDED VOICE: This is the Criterion cinema bringing you details of the very best in screen entertainment in North London. On Screen 1 we have the adult, action-packed adventure thriller *Raw Deal* starring Arnold Swarzenegger. Performances are at 2.45, 5.15, and 7.45. Showing on Screen 2 is *Crocodile Dundee II* with Paul Hogan. This wonderful comedy has performances at 3.00, 5.30 and 8.00. Finally, on Screen 3 another chance to see that romantic classic, *A Room With A View*, with performances at 3.45 and 8.15. May we remind patrons that smoking is only permitted in Screen 1. All tickets are priced at £2.60, with children half price. This is the end of the recorded announcement.

Answers

	NAME OF FILM	KIND OF FILM	TIMES	SMOKING
SCREEN 1	*Raw Deal*	Adventure thriller	2.45 5.15 7.45	Yes
SCREEN 2	*Crocodile Dundee II*	Comedy	3.00 5.30 8.00	No
SCREEN 3	*A Room with a View*	Romantic classic	3.45 8.15	No
Prices:	Adults – £2.60 Children – £1.30			

2 Jeff and Emma decide what to do

In Paper 4 there will almost certainly be one multiple choice listening task, with four choices in each case. Here the tasks are made *gradually* more difficult until they finally follow the same format as the exam. In this case, students have a choice of two rather than four possible answers.

Tapescript

JEFF: What would you like to do then?

EMMA: Well, there's not much on TV, is there? Do you fancy a movie?

JEFF: Fine, but I don't feel like going all the way into town.
What's on locally?

EMMA: Well, I rang the Criterion earlier and they've got *Raw Deal* – you remember we saw something about it on TV last week.

JEFF: No, I don't fancy that. Too much blood and guts.

EMMA: I agree. Oh, there's also *A Room With A View*. Why don't we go and see that?

JEFF: We could but I've seen it.

EMMA: Well, so have I.

JEFF: Sorry, I'd forgotten.

EMMA: But it was so good I'd love to see it again.

JEFF: Oh I would too but not just yet. I only saw it a short while ago.

EMMA: OK. How about *Crocodile Dundee II*?

JEFF: *Crocodile Dundee*! Why didn't you say so? I loved the first one.

EMMA: It was all right. Still, I'd rather we went to that than any of the others. There's a performance at eight.

JEFF: Eight! Well, then it's time we left.

EMMA: Don't panic. That's when the performance begins. There'll be adverts and trailers and things before the film actually starts. *Crocodile Dundee* won't start till at least eight-thirty. We've easily got an hour.

JEFF: But I'm starving. I haven't eaten since lunchtime.

EMMA: I haven't either. Let's grab something on the way. A hamburger or something.

JEFF: Right. I'll get my coat. Have you seen the keys to my car?

EMMA: Weren't they on the mantlepiece?

Answers

1A *I don't feel like going all the way into town.*
2B *No, I don't fancy that. Too much blood and guts.*
I agree.
3A *I only saw it a short while ago.*
4A *It was all right.*
5A *We've easily got an hour.*

p.16 LANGUAGE STUDY
It's time .../I'd rather ...

1 Which tenses are used? The point here is that, although the past simple is used in sentences 1D and 2C, we are talking about now/the future.

Answers

1 A It's time to leave for the airport. (*correct*)
 B It's time for us to go to the airport. (*correct*)
 C It's time that we go to the airport. (*wrong*)
 D It's time we went to the airport. (*correct*)
2 A I'd rather go to the theatre. (*correct*)
 B I'd rather that we go to the theatre. (*wrong*)
 C I'd rather we went to the theatre. (*correct*)

The rule the students should be able to work out for themselves is that, if *It's time ...* or *I'd rather ...* are followed directly by a noun or pronoun, then the verb which follows goes into the past simple.

2 Give one or two of the situations to each pair of students. Let them work out the target sentence, and then, having checked that with you, get them to extend the situation backwards and forwards in time to create a short, but more contextualized, dialogue. Students could act out their dialogues in front of each other.

Answers

1 It's time for me to have a holiday./It's time I had a holiday.
2 I'd rather go to a disco./I'd rather we went to a disco.
3 It's time for you to go to bed.
 It's time you went to bed.
4 I'd rather take a taxi.
 I'd rather we took a taxi.
5 It's time we bought tickets./I'd rather we bought the tickets now.
6 I'd rather walk/take a taxi.
 I'd rather Simon/I drove.
7 I'd rather we had Thai food.
8 It's time we finished this exercise!

p.17 LANGUAGE STUDY
Short replies

To be tried individually, then checked in pairs. Having sorted out the rules in small groups, go round the class making quick-fire statements to which students must give appropriate short replies, e.g. *I can't stand football.*

Answers

1 A 4; B 7; C 8; D 1; E 2; F 3; G 5; H 6

2 We use *so* and *too* when the structure of the stimulus, i.e. the first sentence, is **positive**. *So* comes at the beginning of the reply, and the subject and auxiliary verb which follow are inverted, e.g.
STIMULUS: I like Jane.
So I do. (*wrong*)
So I like. (*wrong*)
So do I. (*correct*)

Too is used after the subject followed by the auxiliary verb, e.g.
STIMULUS: I like Jane.

I	do	too.
subject	*aux.*	*+ too*

Neither comes at the beginning of an answer which is agreeing with a negative statement and *either* comes at the end, e.g.
STIMULUS I can't stand cabbage.
Neither can I.
I can't either.

When students are moving around the class to find another student with similar opinions on the question-naire, make sure that they use statements rather than questions to initially describe their feelings about the various forms of entertainment, e.g. *I really love sunbathing* to which another student will be able to respond with an appropriate short reply.

p.17 SPEAKING
An evening out

To focus attention briefly on the *Useful Language* before starting the activity, put the following sentences on the blackboard with gaps which students together must try and complete appropriately, without reference to their books. Point out that the context is *An Evening Out*.
What . . . . you like . . . . do?
Why . . . . we . . . . to the disco?
. . . . have a hamburger instead.
How . . . . eating out?
Do . . . . fancy . . . . to the cinema?

When students have attempted to complete the gaps, then let them refer to their books.
   For the actual discussion of how to spend their evening you may wish to remind students that should they have to do this kind of activity in the exam it is important that all students participate fully and use as wide a range of language as possible. In order to stimulate discussion you may want to give out the short role cards given here. You can photocopy these cards.

You hate all modern music, particularly when it is played so loud that you can't hear what anyone is saying – which it normally is!

You have recently become very concerned about the nature of the food that you and other people eat. You are shocked by the amount of 'rubbish' that we all consume on a daily basis – it is very important for you that you eat healthily!

You have had a hard week at work and you really just want to do something as relaxing as possible. In general you don't like sport and are not an ener-getic person by any means, but this is especially true tonight!

Although you do have £12 to spend, you are actually trying very hard to save as much money as you can to buy a ring for your boy/girlfriend. However, for the moment, this is a secret. Try and spend as little as possible when you go out tonight!

Before beginning the discussion, make sure the students understand exactly what they have to do and then let them get on with the activity with as little interference as possible. Make a note of mistakes around the target language of expressing preference and agreeing so that you can follow up the activity with a brief 'correction spot'.
   To conclude this activity, one way of getting feedback might be for each group to describe the 'programme' they have finally decided for themselves and at the same time try and persuade you, the teacher, to come with *their* group by *selling* the positive features of the programme they have worked out.

pp.18–19 reading
Fiction to capture the imagination

1 This pre-reading discussion should allow you to hear just how much vocabulary associated with the topic of books and reading the students know.

2 Answers
1D *London Match* is a thriller.
2B *Hollywood Husbands* is light reading.
3C *Family and Friends* is quite serious.
4A *Foundation and Earth* is science fiction.

3 Encourage students to justify their choices, where appropriate, using **keen** on, **can't stand** and so on.

4 The point of this exercise is to show that some-times it is quite easy to deduce the meaning of words from context, but that it may not always be possible! At the end let the students argue out and justify across the class their ideas from the texts. Perhaps nominate one student to be the final dictionary arbiter to decide cases which remain in dispute.

Answers
1 charts = c (*records*)
2 quest = b (*search*)
3 sizzling = a (*speeding*)
4 raciest = b (*exciting*)
5 probes = b (*digs*)
6 veneer = c (*surface*)
7 defected = c (*left*)
8 rock = a (*shake*)

p. 19 USE OF ENGLISH

If your class would enjoy it, you could set these two exercises as a mini-competition – the first team with all correct answers 'wins'!

1 Answers
1 author;   2 library;   3 fiction;   4 shelf;
5 biography

2 Answers

1 look up; 2 looking forward; 3 looking;
4 look after; 5 looking out for

p.20 LANGUAGE STUDY
Past simple or present perfect?

1 Amongst other things, the aim of this exercise is to act as a diagnostic test to see whether your students can sort out when to use the past simple and the present perfect, and how much remedial work will be necessary in this area. Give students about a minute to do the first task.

Answer
7 (author, photographer, waiter, advertising man, railway clerk, art student, comic strip writer)

2 Let students take their time, working in groups, on this exercise. Rather than going through the answers immediately, we would suggest that, having worked through the three *When we use the present perfect* exercises, students could go back to the Len Deighton text in pairs/small groups and see if they want to change any of their original ideas. Where they are happy with their choice and it is present perfect, students should decide which of the categories of use it corresponds to.

Answers
1 has lead; 2 has been writing; 3 has also been (*note position of* **also**); 4 was born; 5 took; 6 did;
7 was; 8 came; 9 went; 10 worked;
11 was; 12 became; 13 produced;
14 Following; 15 returning; 16 went;
17 has lived/been living; 18 was; 19 has written;
20 has he written (*note inversion after* **not only**);
21 has also written

pp.20–21 LANGUAGE STUDY
When we use the present perfect

1 Past simple or present perfect

We use the present perfect to talk about the **indefinite past.** *He has been a photographer* is an example of this use. When we use this tense, there is no reference to *when*, and so the addition of *five years ago* makes it wrong. In this case, we would have to use the past simple, i.e. *He was a photographer five years ago.*

In the second pair of sentences, we are talking about a period that began and finished in the past, and so we cannot use the present perfect which, generally, expresses some kind of connection to the present.

2 Different uses of the present perfect
Answers
A 2; B 4; C 1; D 3

3 Present Perfect simple or continuous

Students should now be able to go through the Len Deighton biography and be able to fully explain which uses of the present perfect are being employed, e.g.
3 *has also been* – happened in the past but we do not know when, 17 *has lived/has been living* – started in the past and is still going on now.

4 Adverbs and word order

After the correct orders have been sorted out, encourage students to think about what exactly they were getting wrong, if anything. Were there consistent mistakes? You may want to give some rules/guidelines to help. (See Sections 211 and 579 *Practical English Usage* (1980), M. Swan, OUP.) Weaker classes may need further work in this area.

Answers
1 She has not spoken to him for ten years.
2 They have just had their house decorated.
3 I have never had such a wonderful meal before.
4 Have you seen that movie yet?
5 She has never been to a musical.
6 Are they still waiting or have they already left?
7 Has she ever eaten this kind of food before?
8 Has he not ever seen the film? (→ Hasn't he ...)

p.21 PRONUNCIATION
Sentence stress

1 Establish the idea of the telegram and the charge per word. Get students to reduce the target sentence to telegram proportions before looking in their books. Then let them check to see how closely their version resembles the book's. Students then attempt to match sentence to message and then try pronouncing the target sentence with correct sentence stress and expression, e.g. 1 with a *horrified* intonation pattern. Having practised this a little, put students in pairs to try and construct mini-dialogues to demonstrate different contexts for the different types of sentence stress – the more humorous the better. This can also be done for the second sentence *You might have killed him.*

Answers
1 C; 2 A; 3 B

2 Tapescript and Answers

A He's been living in France.

B He's been writing books for ages.

C What have you done to my car?

D How long have you been a dancer?

E How long have you been learning English?

F It's late. Where have you been?

G I've been trying to phone.

When students attempt to imitate the sentence stress patterns, you could put them in pairs with the second student trying to respond appropriately to the particular sentence stress pattern, e.g.

STUDENT A He's been living in **France.**
STUDENT B Funny. I was sure it was Belgium.

p.21 SPEAKING
Role play

Put the students together initially in small groups of As and Bs: As to think through different questions they might ask; Bs to look through and understand the given information on p. 28 and possibly invent more. Monitor carefully and be sure that the students are 100% clear about the situation before they start the interview.
Pair up As and Bs – if possible, get interviewers to come in from outside the classroom *in character*. This helps to establish the new situation in the minds of the students.

pp.22–23 READING
Star quality

1 The idea behind this particular pre-reading activity is to encourage students to generate their own interest and objectives for reading the text. They will probably need a little prompting.

Put everything students know or think they know about Michael Jackson on the blackboard and also further information that students would like to know. Having set a time limit, let students read for the answers to their questions.

2 Two choices only. This is providing a slow build-up to the four choices of the exam. Some of the choices are difficult and will alert the students to the types of tricks which are used in the examination. In feedback, stress that a close reading of the text is essential. Tell the students that they have to pretend they are lawyers!

Answers
1B Just because he operated a crane, it doesn't necessarily mean he worked in construction. He could have worked in the docks or in another kind of industry.
2B The writer is just guessing that the house was crowded. He does not know this for a fact.
3A He made $5 million for a Pepsi Cola advertisement.

4B *Pure air* is not necessarily *fresh air.*
5B Our knowledge of Michael Jackson *outside* of the text may tell us that he has had operations to change his appearance. *Within* the text, however, all the writer says is that it is difficult to believe his appearance has changed naturally and that it looks as though he has had operations. It doesn't say that he actually has.

Extension
You may wish to let students underline a limited number of words that they would like to know the meaning of in the text. Give them time to identify their words and then in groups of four they should either explain the meanings to each other where one person knows it *or* attempt to deduce from context. After a few minutes of this, any remaining problems should be dealt with in open class.

3 Discussion points

Here are three free speaking activities based on the *Discussion points:*
1 If students have enjoyed doing the last interview role play, then here is another opportunity – this time students could change roles, i.e. the student who was previously the interviewer becomes Michael Jackson.
2 This could be set up as a debate with pairs of students arguing for or against the motion *It's great to be famous.* If you want to organize this as a full-scale debate in front of the whole class, then it would probably be as well to get two pairs of students to prepare opposing positions before the lesson of the actual debate. (As there is generally a discursive composition set in Paper 2, you may wish to follow this activity up with written homework on the same theme.)
3 The third discussion point lends itself better to a round table discussion perhaps chaired by the teacher.

p.23 USE OF ENGLISH
Changing verbs to nouns

This could be set up as a competition between groups with one point for the correct form of each answer and one point for correct pronunciation (especially stress). Don't forget to tell students that it is important to record vocabulary items with difficult forms together with their stress in their vocabulary records.

Answers
1 performance;   2 encouragement;
3 arrangement;   4 entertainment;   5 advertising;
6 advertisement;   7 competition;   8 competitors;
9 photography;   10 collector;   11 collections

p.24 VOCABULARY
Phrasal verbs with *take*

1 Answers
A 6;   B 4;   C 5;   D 1;   E 3;   F 2

2 Answers
1 off;   2 on;   3 to;   4 over;   5 after;   6 up

Extension
After the two written exercises, you may want to ask students to respond to the following questions in small groups:
- Can you take any famous people off? (Demonstrate it!)
- Who do you take after in your family? In what ways?
- If you could take over the running of this school/country, how would you change things?
- Have you taken on anything new recently? If so, what and why?

p.24–25 WRITING

1 Start by recalling the work done on informal letters done in Unit 1, e.g. *lay-out, useful phrases*. Then let students order the letter and also sort it into appropriate paragraphs. Students check their ideas together as they finish. Encourage them to justify their particular order by reference to discourse markers. The correct order is printed on p.28 of the Coursebook.

Answer
The correct order is 6, 3, 4, 7, 12, 8, 11, 5, 9, 10, 2, 1.

2 Understanding the organization of the letter
1 You'll be sorry to hear …
2 Incidentally, by the way, anyway.
3 I am really sorry …
4 What's more …
5 Would you like to …
6 Guess what!

3 Changing the subject study note
This refers back to 2 in exercise 2. Ask students to assess whether there are any differences in the function of each expression. Then let them read the explanation.

4 One approach is to divide students into pairs, then allocate half the pairs situation 1 and the other half situation 2. Set a time limit to write their letters and at the end of this time you should act as 'postman' and 'deliver' all the letters to the pairs who were writing for the other situation. Then in the same pairs students read and answer the letters they have received. Finally, deliver the second batch of letters for students to read.

During the activity you should monitor, helping students with any problems and checking that the target words and expressions highlighted in exercise 2 are being correctly used. The third situation could be set for homework.

p.25 USE OF ENGLISH
Transformation exercise

Let students attempt this individually at first, then confer and, if there is still disagreement, refer them back to the appropriate section in the unit.

Answers
1 It's time we turned on the TV.
2 I prefer westerns to thrillers.
3 I'd rather we cooked than ate out.
4 Nobody has bought his record player yet.
5 It's years since she (last) appeared live.
6 The last time we saw this quiz show was two months ago.
7 The aerial hasn't been repaired yet.
8 Michael has been singing/a singer since he was small.
9 It's 15 years since that soap opera started.
10 It's the first time I've seen her at this disco.

p.26 USE OF ENGLISH

1 Get students to brainstorm all the different hobbies they know and write them on the blackboard. Elicit the correct spelling. Focus in on stamp-collecting – ask students to suggest why they think this is such a popular hobby. If anyone in the class collects stamps, let them explain what motivates them.

Answers
1 along;   2 about;   3 building;   4 up;   5 had;
6 really;   7 so;   8 a;   9 to;   10 immediately;
11 mysterious;   12 specialize;   13 one;
14 enjoyment;   15 must;   16 share;   17 either;
18 number;   19 come;   20 Just

3 Writing

Prior to the actual writing, give students five to ten minutes to prepare a speech extolling the virtues of a hobby either which they have or which you give them. It might be more interesting to give students fairly out-of-the-ordinary hobbies, e.g. *collecting used matches, walking backwards*! After time for preparation, put students in small groups of three or four to give their speech – have a strict time limit of two minutes for each speech after which they change round. At the end, after everyone has made their speech, the group should agree on which was the most amusing or interesting and summarize it for the whole class. For homework, students should plan and then write out the speech they gave.

p.26–28 USE OF ENGLISH

Let students quickly look through the programmes for any vocabulary they are not sure about. Once this has been sorted out, in small groups they can decide how *they* would most fairly divide up the viewing if they were all sharing one TV. Then they should look at the Smith family's preferences and together decide if the example answer is good or not. After time for consideration, elicit any suggestions for changes from the different groups in open class and put them on the blackboard. Where groups disagree about changes, let them argue it out with justifications across the class. What should come out of the discussion is that the answer is too short and is unfair to some members of the family, James Smith in particular! There are some good things about it too. Most of the other family members would be satisfied: Granny can watch most of her favourite programmes and Eileen can see *Vista* which is all about animal experiments. Also, the answer states that Jason must not stay up after midnight. As said earlier, it is unfair to James. In addition, the answer should discuss the fact that Jason's teacher has recommended that the class should watch the new dramatization of *Oliver Twist*.

Finally let students read the improved version on p.28 and discuss in what ways it is better.

UNIT 3

Survival

Possible lesson organization

L1		
	SPEAKING	pp.29–30
	READING	The remarkable story of Jan Little, pp.30–31
	*VOCABULARY	Phrasal verbs using **give**, p.32
	*LANGUAGE STUDY	**in case** and **so that**, pp.32–33
	LISTENING	Survival games, p.40

L2		
	SPEAKING	Discussing a photograph, p.35
	*USE OF ENGLISH	Gap-filling, p.35
	WRITING	Treating snake bites exs. 1–2, p.36
	USE OF ENGLISH	Dialogue completion exs. 1–3, pp.37–38
	Homework	
	WRITING	Treating snake bites ex. 3, p.36
	USE OF ENGLISH	Dialogue completion ex. 4, p.38

L3		
	LISTENING	Surviving in cold weather, p.33
	*USE OF ENGLISH	Word formation with **live** and **die**, p.34
	PRONUNCIATION	Voicing word endings, p.34
	SPEAKING	Discussing texts, p.39
	LANGUAGE STUDY	Ability, p.39
	Homework	
	WRITING up class composed *hero* story (see *Extension* p.20 of this book)	

* These are the items that are most easily done at home if classroom time is short.

pp.29–30 SPEAKING

This speaking activity will give you an opportunity to see how well the students can work together to solve a fairly complex problem involving both logic and English. If students are going to take the group inter-view option in the final examination, it will be impor-tant to check that the 'chemistry' between different group members is just right.

1 Find out if anyone has done any rock-climbing or mountaineering. What was it like? Would other people in the class like to do it? Why/Why not? What would the class consider to be vital equipment when going

rock-climbing? Elicit all the vocabulary in the exercise. Set the scene by reading the introduction out loud to the class. Then let the students complete the sentences in pairs and go over any grammatical problems in open class.

Answers
1 few/none;   2 most;   3 both;   4 all/any;
5 little/any;   6 few;   7 much;   8 no/all;
9 many;   10 every

2 Sort out any problematic vocabulary before discussion gets under way as it is necessary for students to have fully understood the information contained in the completion exercise on p.29 as well as the Extra Points to consider before embarking on this task. Put students in groups of three or four to sort out a new climbing team. At the end, each group should present their solution with the reasons for it. The other groups listen and then vote on the best solution – each team awarding three points for the best, two for the second and one for the third. No team can vote for itself!

Suggested solution

All the nationalities need each other. The Russians have rope and food, the Chinese a large tent, and the Americans ice-axes without which the final part of the climb would be impossible. They must co-operate in order to conquer the peak before the Canadians.

As the American is badly injured, the Chinese doctor should stay with him while one of the Russians goes down to base camp for further help. The doctor and the injured climber would stay in the two-man tent and wait for help to arrive. The doctor will keep the medical equipment and a saucepan. It would use up too many supplies to take the injured man down the mountain.

The remaining four climbers should try to get to just below the final 200 metres and camp. They will have the four-man tent and the rest of the supplies including the rope and ice-axes. The following day one of the Americans should stay at the camp while the other three, with their ice-axes, attempt the final part of the climb. As the Russian is the best climber, he/she should lead the way. The rope will probably be too short to reach the top so he/she may have to do the final 25 metres on his/her own. He/She should, however, put all three nations' flags on the peak as a sign of international co-operation and peace. The climb back to Base Camp will take 1½ days. So 4 climb-ers x (2 days + 1½ days) = 14 days' supplies.

---

pp.30–31 READING
The remarkable story of Jan Little

1 Put the following vocabulary items on the black-board and let students in pairs predict the content of the story that they will subsequently read: *immigrants, jungle, hardships, blind, snakes, bucket, rope, matches, help.*

Students should then read to see how closely their story resembles the one in the book and answer the questions on the page.

Answers
1 They made their home on a hill by a river in the jungle on the border between Venezuela and Brazil.
2 Life was hard.
3 The cause of their sickness remains unknown but could have been a kind of malaria.
4 The first time she had to leave the hut was to remove her daughter's body.
5 She overcame her problems through a mixture of her determination to live and practical planning, e.g. getting water from the river and marking her trail with pieces of cloth.
6 Her survival is remarkable because she was blind, deaf and weak, and had relied almost entirely on her husband and daughter before their deaths. In addition, the jungle was a dangerous place for someone in such a condition.

2

1B *As a child she suffered from poor vision ...*
2B *... their nearest neighbour was a five-day canoe trip away.* It is unlikely you would make a reference to a canoe trip without a river nearby.
3C *... until 30th December 1979 when disaster struck ... an awful disease which ... It may have been a kind of malaria but we're not sure.*
4B *... she had to make her way down to the river and the store. .. was situated at the top of a hill.*
5A *Jan realised that survival depended on her being able to reach the store hut.* The trail was not made of pieces of cloth, only marked by them.
6A *Six weeks after Rebecca's death, Harry died.* Help came *four and a half months* after Rebecca's death so she was without human company for 18 weeks minus six weeks equals 12 weeks.

3 Answers

1 brought up; 2 rural; 3 vision; 4 give up;
5 homesteaders; 6 border; 7 crops; 8 hardships;
9 go down with; 10 crawl; 11 drag; 12 live off;
13 helpless; 14 run out of; 15 steep

Extension
Put students in pairs. One is Jan Little and retells the story but changes five small details from the original story. The other student listens, asks questions and notes down the five differences.

p.32 VOCABULARY
Phrasal verbs using *give*

The aim of this exercise is to introduce students to the multiplicity of meanings that some phrasal verbs have. It will also help them familiarize themselves with how different meanings appear in dictionary entries.
With the first of the two examples of *give up* it is being used with meaning 1 of the dictionary definitions. The second has meaning 2.

Answers
1 give out – 1
2 gave away – 1
3 gave off
4 gave up – 5
5 give up – 2
6 I give in – 1
7 gave away – 3
8 give up – 1
9 gives back

Extension
After completing the exercise, put the students in pairs to work on a short dialogue with the aim of including as many phrasal verbs from *give* as possible. Set a time limit of about ten minutes after which the pairs should act out their dialogue in front of the class to see who has managed to include the most phrasal verbs.

p.32–33 LANGUAGE STUDY
in case and *so that*

1/2 Put the following prompt on the blackboard:
She took an umbrella in case ...
She took an umbrella so that ...
Ask students to complete the sentences. Put up all correct possibilities that students come up with. From this, let them in small groups deduce the construction and meaning of the two forms. Then read the explanations in the book to check.

3 Pre-teach the vocabulary which may cause problems, e.g. a *jack, puncture.*

Answers
1 You should insure your house in case you have a fire.
2 The film star wore dark glasses so that he wouldn't be recognized / nobody would recognize him.
3 She packed the glasses carefully so that they wouldn't get broken in the post.
4 You should always have a jack and carry a spare tyre in case you have a puncture.
5 Take this serum in case a snake bites you / you get bitten by a snake.
6 The thief wore gloves so that he wouldn't / didn't leave fingerprints.
7 The notices in the hotel are in seven languages so that everyone can understand them.

8 You had better take traveller's cheques so that if they get stolen you'll be able to get some more.

4 To stimulate the discussion, you may wish to divide the class into two groups: over-protective parents and ultra laid-back youngsters going on the camping holiday. After time for the two sides to decide what they think it will be necessary for them to take, put pairs of young people and parents together to negotiate what is actually necessary to take and why.

p.33 LISTENING

1 Focus students' attention on the photo and ask them to guess the situation and what probably happened. Ask students if they have ever been in a similar situation. If so, what happened exactly. Then put students in pairs to discuss their survival plans and then select one or two to give their ideas in open class.

2/3 Surviving in the snow

Tapescript

PRESENTER: Now, I'd like to move on to the next item. The weather certainly seems to have taken a turn for the worse and it looks like we're in for some heavy snowfalls in the next few days. Now, of course, every year there are cases of motorists who break down and get caught out in really bad weather. Tragically, some die and this is even more tragic when we consider that most of these deaths could be avoided. Now we have in the studio this evening Julie Mitchell from the Canadian Automobile Club and she's going to tell us how to stay alive if we get caught out in the snow and our car breaks down. Hi, Julie.

JULIE: Hi.

PRESENTER: So what should we do?

JULIE: Well, the first thing that you should remember is that your car is your most important piece of survival equipment you have if you get caught in a drift. So don't leave it unless you can actually see the place you want to get to. People have died when they needn't have because they have gotten impatient, left their cars and got lost in the snow.

PRESENTER: So, rule number one is stay in your car unless you can see where you're going.

JULIE: Your destination.

PRESENTER: Right. Anything else we should remember?

JULIE: Oh, certainly! First of all, use your common sense. If you have to drive and know you're going to hit bad weather, make sure you have blankets, a sleeping bag and a shovel in case you have to dig yourself out, and ideally food and hot drinks.

PRESENTER: Is there anything we can do to help ourselves if we're stuck, apart from keep warm, that is?

JULIE: Oh, sure. You've got to keep warm but you've also got to keep the car well ventilated – there have been cases of drivers suffocating in their cars – so

have the window on the side away from the wind open a little, say half an inch or so.

PRESENTER: Ok. What about using the car heater to keep warm?

JULIE: Oh, I'm glad you asked me about this because this can be fatal unless you take extreme care. The risk of death from exhaust fumes is high. The cold takes hours to kill you but exhaust fumes can kill you in a matter of minutes. Before you run your engine, make sure the exhaust is competely free from snow. Otherwise, the fumes will escape into the car. Anyway, only run the engine for ten minutes every hour and every time make sure the exhaust is free.

PRESENTER: Any final tip?

JULIE: Yes. If you know you're setting off in bad weather, ring up your destination just in case something happens on the way. That way, if you're late, your friends will know something is wrong and will be able to tell the police to go out and look for you.

PRESENTER: Thanks Julie for coming in and I hope our listeners out there... .

Answers
1 your car
2 stay in your car unless you can see where you are going.
3 a sleeping bag
4 a shovel
5 food and hot drinks
6 half an inch or so
7 side away from the wind
8 a matter of minutes.
9 10 minutes
10 ring up your destination.

p.34 USE OF ENGLISH

Before attempting these three exercises, let students brainstorm all the different words coming from the root words *live/die*, and also any associated phrasal verbs and expressions. Put all correct ideas on the blackboard and then let them attempt exercises 1–3.

1 Answers

1 alive; 2 life; 3 live; 4 lively; 5 life (time);
6 lives

2 Answers

1 dying; 2 deadly; 3 death; 4 dead; 5 deathly

3 Answers

1 dying for; 2 live on; 3 dying out; 4 live down;
5 life, death

Extension
You may wish to follow this up with a discussion or debate around the subject of euthanasia.

p.34 PRONUNCIATION
Voicing word endings

Answers

voiced	voiceless
live	life
dead	debt
rise	rice
mend	meant
hard	heart
knees	niece
save	safe

Having put the words in the correct columns, you should say one of the words and students identify if it contained a voiced or voiceless sound, indicating A or B. After a few examples like this, let students try it out on each other in pairs.

p.35 SPEAKING
Discussing a photograph

Either discuss the photo in pairs **or** ask each person in the pair to speak continuously for a minute or two in response to the prompts. (In Paper 5 one of the most important things is for candidates to keep talking, not dry up and not give one word answers.) You may like to demonstrate the kind of answer that examiners will be looking for, after students have had a go at it. It may also be worth compiling a list of key vocabulary and useful phrases for this photo on the blackboard before asking students to have another go at describing the photo.

p.35 USE OF ENGLISH

Students should read through the cloze text quickly to see how accurate their predictions about the photo were and then attempt to complete it in pairs.

Answers
1 break; 2 living; 3 all; 4 attract; 5 fewer;
6 most; 7 whose; 8 any; 9 them; 10 that;
11 already; 12 both; 13 by; 14 even;
15 instead; 16 could; 17 in; 18 might; 19 As;
20 spent

p.36 WRITING

1 Ask students to predict what they would do with someone who had just been bitten by a snake. Then skim through the text to see if they had any ideas in common. Then have students try and order the text, checking with a partner and then, if necessary, pairs check together. In the groups of four compile a list of the words and phrases that helped with the ordering.

Answer
The correct order is E, B, D, F, C, A.

2 **Answers**
1 E *Can I have your attention, please?* marks the beginning.
   B *Now, just a few words before I start* – introduction of speech
   D *So* ... links the consequent *object of the exercise* to the stated situation of Fatima having been bitten.
   F *This means* leads to the practical application of having to have *the heart ... higher than the bitten area*, i.e. *we'll have Fatima sitting up.*
   C *As I was saying* continues the advice about how tight the bandage should be.
   A *So, that's how you do it* concludes this introductory explanation.
2 A *Right everyone, can I have your attention, please?*
   B *gather round*
   C Instructions are introduced with *now* and *first of all* and then given using the imperative, e.g. *do all you can, make the victim relax.*
   D *Who would like to have a go?*

3   Students will probably come up with *to begin with, next, after that, afterwards* ...

Extension
In groups of four students take it in turns to act out the scene, changing roles (*demonstrator, victim, onlookers*) each time.

3 This can be set as homework.

pp.37–38 USE OF ENGLISH

This section aims to train learners how to approach the open dialogue question. More specificially, it goes through the following steps:
• It shows students the type of error which is often made by candidates attempting this question. (*Expert on snake bites interview*)
• It provides practice in identifying errors. (*Carlo and the accommodation officer*)
• It gives some free practice in trying the exercise type independently.

1 Let students analyse the bad version and consider the teacher's comments. Then look at the model version on p.41 critically, picking out the particularly good features and seeing if there is still anything they would change. From all this preparatory work as a class, students should come up with a checklist of how to approach/things to remember about the dialogue completion exercise.

2 Students should look to see if they have covered all the points mentioned.

3 Let students work on this exercise in pairs for about ten minutes. Then team them up with another pair to see if they agree in what they think is wrong with it. As a change of activity, you may wish to get students to act out the Barbara/Carlo dialogue when you have agreed on an acceptable version.

Possible commentary on Barbara/Carlo dialogue

My roomate is a horrible boy.

- logical but it would be more natural to say *My roommate is horrible*.

He smokes always.

- grammatical error: You should say *He's always smoking* or *He smokes in our room*.

- accuracy error: spelling of *roomate*, needs double 'm'.

He said bad things to me.

- logical: *He swore at me* would be better.

Yes, I would like to change.

- quite logical, but the answer is too long. *Yes, I would is* enough. Apart from this, there isn't anything to prompt Barbara's reply. Carlo should add something extra like *I would like to have a single room*.

That's too expensive.

- logical but inappropriate. This would sound very rude! *I'm afraid that's rather too expensive for me* would be better. Carlo could also say *Do you have anything else?*

O.K.

- illogical: you could say *That sounds better* followed by *How far is it from the school?*

It is too far.

- again, this is illogical as it doesn't take into account the reply or the rest of the conversation. It also sounds rude in its directness. *It's a little far, but I'd still like to see the room* would be better.

I prefer later on.

- logical but wrong grammar *I'd prefer to/rather see it later on*.

So, in this answer, the student starts quite well but then loses the thread of the argument.

4 Answers

1 The brown/red/green ones?
2 What size are you/do you take?
3 How do these feel?
4 I'm afraid we've just sold the last pair.
5 Would you like to try on something else?
6 You could always visit our Castle Street branch.

p.39 SPEAKING
Discussing texts

Divide the class into three groups, allocating one text to each group. Groups study their text, sort out all unknown vocabulary (by deducing from context, consulting dictionaries, asking the teacher) and discuss the three prompt questions. Then put students into new groups of three with each member of the new groups having read a different text. Students take it in turns to explain the text *they* read and their ideas about the context it might originally have been found in.

Suggested answers

A 1 a hijacked plane
  2 the narrator
  3 a written text – a spy/adventure thriller
B 1 search for a capsized fishing boat
  2 newsreader
  3 radio/TV news broadcast
C 1 two brothers on the run from the sheriff
  2 the brothers
  3 probably the dialogue from a TV western – note the incorrect English.

p.39 LANGUAGE STUDY
Ability

1 In the same groups of three, students should find all the different expressions of ability and complete the Language Study activities.

Answers

1 A He *could* control ...
   Blond *was able to* get out ...
   ... *managed* to force it open
 B They have *succeeded in* rescuing ...
 C ... *you'll be able to* have ...
   ... you *could* walk for miles.
   You *can* do it.
2 We say Blond *was able to* get out because this describes the ability to do something on a particular occasion. *Could* describes a more general ability.
3 manage + infinitive, e.g. *We managed to do it.*
  succeed + in + verb + -ing, e.g. *We succeeded in doing it.*

2 Answers

1 A or B; 2 A or B; 3 B; 4 A; 5 A; 6 B; 7 B

Extension
Get students to sit in a circle and tell them you are together going to create an adventure involving a hero, capture and escape. Then begin the story by saying *James Blond was on his way to the airport. It looked like it was going to be another difficult assignment.* Students, in turn, add a sentence each to the story, preferably being as dramatic as possible!
  This should give an opportunity for students to include the target structures as well as being quite a

fun speaking activity. As a follow-up, students may be asked to write up the complete story for homework. If the story does not get finished in class time, they can finish it at home. (It can be fun to stick up the final compositions around the class for students to compare versions.)

p.40 LISTENING
Survival games

Ask students to look at the photo and say what they think is happening. Then make sure they read through the questions and alternative answers before listening. Let students compare answers after the first listening and then play the cassette again for them to check.

Tapescript
MIKE: Well, I just sort of watched the telly really. Did a bit of laundry. Had a drink. That was about it.

PHIL: I don't blame you. The weather was awful, wasn't it? That drizzle. Cold as well ... I was fed up. What did you do, Kim?

KIM: Well, I had quite a good time, actually. I went on one of these, you know, survival games weekends.

MIKE: You what!

KIM: You must have heard of them. These survival games.

MIKE: What do you do?

KIM: Well, you ... Oh, I'm not going to tell you 'cause you'll only take the mickey.

MIKE and PHIL: No, no. Go ... Tell us. Tell us.

KIM: Do you really want to hear?

MIKE and PHIL: Yeah.

KIM: Well, the idea of it is to capture an enemy flag. You're split into two teams and ... see! I told you. You're laughing already.

MIKE: No, no. Come on. Let's hear the whole lot.

PHIL: You spent the weekend playing soldiers?

KIM: Well, we only had ink pellets. It wasn't real bullets.

PHIL: Ah, pathetic! What happens? You fire them at other people?

KIM: Yeah, you have about 40 minutes. It lasts 40 minutes and you've got to try and – well, like I said – capture the...

PHIL: Isn't that a bit dangerous? Well, what do you fire them at?

KIM: No, no. You get this visor thing to wear to protect your eyes.

MIKE: What and bang bang you're dead?

KIM: Yeah, then they're out once you've got them. Once you've been hit by an ink pellet. It's good fun. Well, it's great. It's better than sitting around watching telly. I was out in the open air, running around.

MIKE: I don't know about that.

PHIL: I don't know. It's quite nice being out.

KIM: Yeah, it was very invigorating.

MIKE: What were the others like then? Were they all little kids playing Cowboys and Indians?

KIM: No they were fairly normal people. Young. There was more men than women which was nice. It was just innocent fun for the weekend. It was good.

PHIL: Did you go with anybody, like did you go with a friend or anything?

KIM: Yeah, I went with Tricia, a girl I worked with.

MIKE: Ah, Tricia! She was doing it as well.

KIM: Yeah. We just thought we'd try it.

PHIL: I can't imagine her doing it.

KIM: We're going to go again. We really enjoyed it. You should come along.

PHIL: Kept stopping to do her make-up.

MIKE: World War Three. You going to do it again?

KIM: Yes!

Answers
1C *the idea of it is to capture an enemy flag.*
2C *What and bang bang you're dead. Yeah ...*
3C *It's great ... I was out in the open air.*
4A *Ah, pathetic ... Were they all little kids playing Cowboys and Indians?*
5C *No, they were fairly normal people. Young.*

2 *Discussion points* to be considered in small groups.

Units 1–3 Revision crossword

Across

1 The usual follow-up to a question (6)
5 (*Across and Down*) It used to be ideal. (4, 7)
7 Not at all often, in fact (6)
8 I neither like . . . . dislike opera. (3)
10 Why don't you get . . . . with him? He's really nice. (2)
12 I decided to learn English . . . . that I would have a chance of getting a better job later. (2)
13 He's very good at taking . . . . famous people. (3)
14 I think all of us should have stayed in the car and waited for help, shouldn't . . . .? (2)
15 We had completely given . . . . hope of ever being found. (2)
16 Royal hesitation (2)
18 A short article (1)
19 It's no good having a strong one of these. No one will understand you! (6)
21 The working members on board (4)
22 A letter of surprise (2)
23 I knew you would take . . . . him straight away. He's your sort of person. (2)
27 It comes to us all eventually. (5)
28 I've been studying English . . . . 10 years now. (3)
30 Morning time (2)
32 He's the only one . . . . really has any serious rock-climbing experience. (3)
33 To . . . . or not to . . . .? A very famous question. (2)
34 These could be considered as Home Sweet Home for the campers. (5)

Down

1 Between seats (5)
2 All over the place (10)
3 Brief thanks (2)
4 I'm staying . . . . the Piccadilly Hotel. (2)
5 See 5 across.
6 It's the greatest . . . . on earth! (4)
8 There's . . . . point asking him. He can't stand the cinema! (2)
9 I'm tired . . . . being the one who always has to clean up! (2)
11 . . . . of us are interested in survival games. (7)
17 Regarding, concerning (2)
19 A short advertisement (2)
20 Totally negative (2)
21 Often accompanies a bad cold (5)
24 You know it's remarkable how many different ways they . . . . after their mother. (4)
25 I bought the tickets for the late performance so . . . . we wouldn't have to hurry our meal. (4)
26 It looks like we've run out . . . . milk again. (2)
29 We're going to give . . . . all the presents after lunch. (3)
31 A: I'm always late for appointments.
   B: . . . . too. (2)

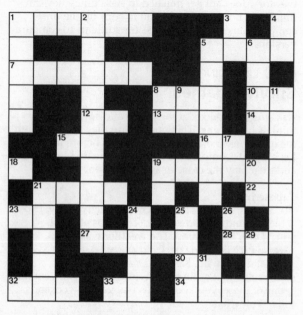

UNIT 4

Storytelling

Possible lesson organization

L1		
	SPEAKING	Stories from child-hood, p.42
	LANGUAGE STUDY	Past tenses, pp.42–43
	PRONUNCIATION	Past tenses, p.44
	*USE OF ENGLISH	Sleep, p.44
	LISTENING	An alternative Cinder-ella, p.44
	Homework	
	Write a traditional story from your country or a modern version of one.	

L2		
	WRITING	Gelert 1, p.45
	*USE OF ENGLISH	Gelert 2, p.45
	READING	Dick Whittington, pp.48–49
	WRITING	Understanding style, p.50
	LISTENING	Cinderella and Dick Whittington, pp.50–51
	Homework	
	VOCABULARY	Time expressions, p.48
	READING	Dirty Harry, p.51

L3		
	LANGUAGE STUDY	The grammar of phrasal verbs, pp. 46–47
	*VOCABULARY	Phrasal verbs p.46
	LISTENING	A tall story, p.52
	WRITING	The narrative compo-sition, pp. 52–53
	Homework	
	WRITING	ex. 2:3 *Fire* composi-tion, p.53

* *These are the items that are most easily done at home if classroom time is short.*

p.42 SPEAKING

Get students to describe the illustration and then see how many of the stories are familiar to them. In small groups each student should try and recall *one* favourite story they remember being told as a child. In multilingual classes it can be interesting to see in what ways the same stories differ from country to country. The illustration shows from left to right *Puss in Boots, Sleeping Beauty, Snow White* and *Tom Thumb*.

pp.42–43 LANGUAGE STUDY
Past tenses

1/2 Find out if anyone knows the story of Little Red Riding Hood and then ask them to summarize it for the class with the other students adding anything that gets missed out or forgotten, or giving alternative versions. Then ask students to read the opening part of the story to see if there are any differences between the class version and the version in the book. When they have done this, students should find examples of the target tenses and in small groups try and analyse *why* each is used when it is. Then they should look through 2 to compare their ideas with the explanations given in the book. Allow time for discussion of any points which are not immediately clear.

3 In the same groups let students work together, ap-plying the rules of 2.

Answers
1 asked; 2 was going; 3 had never seen; 4 told;
5 lived; 6 was; 7 heard; 8 hurried;
9 had forgotten; 10 made; 11 rushed; 12 was;
13 pretended; 14 opened

4 Monitor while this is being done, helping with vo-cabulary but, above all, checking the use of narrative tenses. At the end, let each group read out their ending to compare. (Tell students they do not have to keep to the original version but can create their own ending if they wish.)

Just to remind you how the story goes:
Granny lets the wolf inside, the wolf eats her up and then gets into bed disguising itself as the old lady. Little Red Riding Hood arrives to find 'Granny' lying in bed. 'Granny' says she's unwell and asks the girl to get into bed with her. In the English version their dialogue goes:
'Granny, What big ears you've got.'
'All the better to hear you with, my child.'
'Granny, what big eyes you've got.'
'All the better to see you with.'
'Granny what big teeth you've got.'
'All the better to gobble you up!'
Here the English version of the story ends, but for those of a sensitive disposition you could add that two hunters/woodcutters see the wolf later that day and slay it. When they open the creature up, they find the girl and her grandmother inside none the worse for wear!

p.44 PRONUNCIATION
Past tenses

1 Regular verbs in the past

First let students predict in which columns the verbs belong and then listen to the cassette.

Answers

/d/	/t/	/ɪd/
stayed	asked	waited
carried	promised	decided
contained		invited
frightened		

2 was and were

Go over parts 1 and 2 in open class, then again let them predict the pronunciation of *was/were* **before** listening. Then listen to check.

3 Tapescript and Answers

MAN: Where were you last night?
(*weak*)
WOMAN: I was at the office.
(*weak*)
MAN: Were you?
(*strong*)
WOMAN: Yes, I was. I was working late.
(*strong/weak*)
MAN: You were with Paul!
(*weak*)
WOMAN: No, I wasn't.
(*strong*)
MAN: Yes, you were.
(*strong*)

4

Get students to act out the dialogue – once or twice with scripts and then without, encouraging them each to sound as outraged as possible!

p.44 USE OF ENGLISH

You may want to ask students to quickly brainstorm as many words based on *sleep* as they can think of before completing the exercise.

Answers

1 Sleeping;   2 sleepy;   3 asleep;
4 sleeping pills/tablets;   5 sleeper;   6 sleeping bag;
7 sleepless

p.44 LISTENING
An alternative Cinderella

1

First of all students in pairs try and recall the story of Cinderella. If anyone does not know the story, put them in a group with someone who does and who can explain it to them. Students then read the questions, and listen and check their answers together. Then listen again.

NARRATOR: Once upon a time there were three sisters who lived with their widowed father. The two eldest ran a beauty parlour and a clothes shop. They were both interested in finding a rich husband. The youngest daughter, whose name was Cinderella, looked after the house. Her father had refused to set her up in business as he wanted someone to look after him. Cinderella did not mind too much as she was doing a correspondence course in accountancy and marketing.

One day Cinderella decided to enter a competition in a woman's magazine because it offered some good cash prizes. If she won one of them, it would help her finance the setting-up of her own hamburger restaurant.

Around that time the newspapers were full of stories about a big party that was going to be held at the palace. It was said that the prince, a real playboy, wanted to find a wife and settle down. From the moment they heard about the ball, the two eldest sisters spent days and days trying to make themselves look beautiful. As for Cinderella, she wondered what all the fuss was about and didn't have the slightest interest in going to the ball.

One morning, while she was doing some work for her accountancy course, there was a knock at the door. She opened it and saw an extraordinary woman standing there with a ridiculous looking tiara on her head. The woman, who called herself Fairy Godmother or FG for short, told Cinderella that she'd won first prize in the magazine competition she'd entered.

The prize was a 'charm course' worth hundreds of pounds as well as books and records. Cinderella wasn't really that keen on doing the course but she realized she could probably make a small profit if she sold the prizes. However, in return for the prizes she would have to dress up in lots of fine clothes and be driven to the palace where she'd spend the night at the ball and be photographed for the woman's magazine.

The big day arrived and a shiny Rolls Royce came to pick her up. The man from the car hire firm said he was only on duty until midnight. Moments later a woman arrived bringing a fur coat and a diamond necklace which would be Cinderella's just for the evening. When she turned up at the palace, she noticed that one of the servants was stealing food from the buffet tables. The palace itself was cold and draughty, and the king himself was a man with a sad smile. Cinderella felt sorry for the man and told him why the food was disappearing so fast. The king then told her about his financial problems. He was almost bankrupt and he had organized the party in the hope that he might find a millionaire's daughter for his son. Cinderella suggested lots of ways of making money: reorganizing the kitchens, opening the palace to the public and so on.

By this time it had turned midnight. The car hire man drove away and the woman came to collect her fur coat and necklace. The king showed Cinderella around the palace and they eventually came back to the ballroom where the party was still going on. The prince, who by this time was hopelessly drunk, took one look at Cinderella and asked her to dance. She kicked off her glass slippers, which were killing her, and joined him on the dance floor. Soon afterwards, she left the palace and hitch-hiked home.

The following day the newspapers were full of the big story about the prince who had fallen for a beautiful and mysterious woman who had disappeared. Her glass slippers, which she had left behind, were the only clues that would lead him to her. When Cinderella read the news, she was absolutely furious. Nevertheless, she saw quite a bit of the prince because she started work at the palace as financial adviser. In no time at all the palace was making a profit again. Naturally, Cinderella refused to marry the prince but she did help him cut down on his drinking and involved him in useful social work in the community.

Answers

1 Cinderella's great ambition was to set up her own hamburger restaurant.
2 The king had organized a ball to find a wealthy bride for his lazy son.
3 She went to the ball because she had to go there as a condition of winning the prize in the magazine competition.
4 At midnight the chauffeur drove the car away and someone took the fur coat and necklace.
5 She helped the Royal Family by acting as their financial adviser and making the palace profitable again. She also helped the Prince to cut down on his drinking and involved him in useful social work in the community.

Extension

You may want to say to students that they are going to retell the complete story, but that they have one more chance to listen to the story and take notes if they wish. Then, put students in A/B pairs, the As to retell the story and the Bs to make a note of any information they think their partner has missed. At the end, the Bs tell the As anything they think has been missed. Then both can check the tapescript to see if there was anything they both missed.

2 Let students work on this in groups. (In multilingual classes you may want to put students from the same parts of the world together.) Then nominate one person in each group to relate their story to the rest of the class.

p.45 WRITING

1 Focus students' attention on the illustration and give them two to three minutes to describe it in pairs. Then elicit one sentence of description from each pair, helping with vocabulary as the need arises. Particularly encourage students to predict who the man is, what he is doing and why. Students then read the story to check their ideas and decide on an appropriate title. If they have any problems with vocabulary, make sure they attempt to deduce the meaning of words from context before consulting didictionaries or you.

2 Brainstorm in open class ways of making the story more interesting. Put on the blackboard vocabulary elicited from the class which may be useful. Having given time for students in groups to expand the story, put up each version on the walls of the classroom and let students move round and read them.

An Expanded Version of Brave Gelert

This story is set, many years ago, in Wales, in the Middle Ages. At this time, towards the south of the kingdom, there was a prince whose name was Llewellyn. The prince was a tall, powerfully built young man with long black hair and an equally black moustache. He was well-known in the area for his generosity but he also had a reputation for behaving rather impetuously at times.

The prince lived in a long fertile green valley which had large forests on both sides extending for many miles in each direction. He lived there with the daughter of a local chief whom he had had the good fortune to marry two years before. She had recently had a beautiful baby boy who was now the pride and joy of the young prince.

Of scarcely less importance to the prince was his dog, Gelert, a great shaggy Irish wolfhound. The prince had found him wounded and starving in a nearby forest five years before, and since then the dog had been his constant companion.

One day, shortly after sunrise, the prince decided to go hunting, leaving Gelert to look after the baby. However, while he was away, one of the many ferocious packs of wolves who roamed the land in search of food and were the terror of the area, came out of a nearby wood and ran towards the small wooden cottage where the baby was sleeping. Gelert, however, saw them coming and managed to hide the baby. Having done this he ran outside and fought the wolves, killing two of them but being wounded in the process. Finally the wolves ran off and Gelert, exhausted from the fight, lay down to sleep.

When Llewellyn returned, in the late afternoon, the first thing he saw was the sleeping dog covered in blood. On entering the cottage he also saw that his son's cot was empty and so in a fit of rage, he took his sword and, with a mighty stroke, cut the dog in half while he slept. Just then, he heard the cry of a baby and discovered the hidden child. As he was picking up the infant he happened to notice the two dead wolves lying outside the cottage and then he understood what had really happened.

Full of sadness and remorse for what he had done, he carried Gelert through the howling wind and pouring rain to the top of the highest hill in the region and buried him, placing a pile of stones on the spot to mark the position of the grave.

That spot has survived the test of time and you can still see the pile of stones to this very day.

---

p.45 USE OF ENGLISH

Either set for homework **or** an alternative way of treating this and the previous *Writing* section would be to let half the students in the class work on the *Writing* section and half the students in the class work on the *Use of English* section. When both have had time, put them in A/B pairs, As to relate the original story in their *interesting* version and Bs to explain the *real* situation.

Answers
1 terrible/sad/tragic;   2 few;   3 so;   4 up;
5 hardly;   6 bright;   7 had/once;   8 surprising;
9 popular;   10 what;   11 been;   12 would;
13 actually;   14 Accordingly;   15 his;   16 it;
17 on;   18 from;   19 the;   20 Needless

p.46 VOCABULARY
Phrasal verbs

1 Answers

A 7; B 6; C 4; D 8; E 11; F 9; G 3; H 10; I 1; J 5 (This generally suggests a good relationship with someone.); K 12; L 2

2 Answers

1 find out;   2 came across;   3 told ... off;
4 took ... in;   5 get on with;   6 putting... off;
7 fell for;   8 put up with;   9 turned down;
10 looked after;   11 turned up;   12 set off

3 This could be done as homework.

Extension
Put students in small groups to invent their own story using as many of the phrasal verbs in exercise 1 as they can. At the end they should relate their story to the whole class.

pp.46–47 LANGUAGE STUDY
The grammar of phrasal verbs

Clearly learners can't consciously think about the grammar of phrasal verbs every time they wish to use one or meet one in a text. Indeed, phrasal verbs can be acquired without any kind of formally conscious understanding of how they function. However, it can be useful to know something of the rules governing their use when it comes to the First Certificate examination and, in particular, in order to understand why some answers are right and others wrong in Section A of Paper 1.

1 Transitive and intransitive verbs

Put on the blackboard:
Anne likes.
Anne likes John.
The sun rose.
The sun rose the sky.
He understood.
He understood her.

Ask students to decide which of these sentences are possible and which are not and why. Then ask them to read the explanation and do the task.

Answers
3 rise I;   raise T;   thank T;   understand I, T;
go I;   see I, T;   open T;   laugh I;   arrive I

Note that some verbs can be used either transitively or intransitively.

2 Exploring the grammar of phrasal verbs

Answers
1/2
A
i) correct   ii) wrong   iii) correct
Turn up meaning *arrive* is intransitive. In other words, it cannot take an object. *Late for everything* is a complement which finishes off the sentence, but it is not an object.
B
i) wrong;   ii) correct;   iii) correct;   iv) wrong;
v) correct
The rule one can work out from this is that *tell off* is transitive. What's more, sentences iii) and v) show that it is separable. In other words, an object can be placed between the verb and its particle. The difficulty here is that if a pronoun is used, it must be placed between the verb and particle and not at the end. *Tell off* is transitive and separable.
C
i) wrong;   ii) correct;   iii) wrong;   iv) correct;
v) wrong
Sentence i) is wrong so this tells us that *look after* is transitive; in other words, it must have an object. The other sentences show us that the noun or pronoun have to follow the phrasal verb and that the verb and its particle cannot be split. *Look after* is transitive but inseparable.
D
i) wrong;   ii) wrong;   iii) correct;   iv) correct
Three part phrasal verbs are always transitive and inseparable.

If some students find this activity rather difficult, make sure that they get the basic message: *the most important thing you have to discover when you meet a new phrasal verb is whether it is possible to separate the verb and the particle.*

26

3 On examining the entry for *turn up*, students will notice that not only does it have a number of different meanings, but that its grammar may vary too.

p.48 VOCABULARY
Time expressions

Answers
1 while; 2 during; 3 at the end; 4 for;
5 previously; 6 eventually; 7 whenever;
8 In the meantime; 9 until; 10 Afterwards;
11 in the end; 12 before

pp.48–49 READING
The story of Dick Whittington

1 You may wish to ask students, in pairs, to look at and attempt to describe the pictures **before** reading the story. The correct order of the pictures is C, G, I, F, J, H, E, A, D, B. Students may decide on a slightly different order and should be encouraged to do so if they can justify this from the text.

2
1 once upon a time; 2 once; 3 each time; 4 As;
5 on; 6 so; 7 However; 8 whenever;
9 One day; 10 eventually; 11 Afterwards;
12 Unfortunately; 13 Nevertheless; 14 meanwhile;
15 when; 16 finally; 17 following

3 Here is a list of words and phrases which may cause problems: *orphan, paved, bundle, seek, come by, came across, take pity on someone, took him in, penny, grateful, got on well with, bartered, put up with, edge.*

p.50 WRITING
Understanding style

1 Answers
1 his – the captain's
  he – the captain
  there – the palace
  where – the dining room
  they – the king and the guests
  their – the king's and the guest's
  guest who – the captain
  him – the king
  monarch – the king
  sailor – the captain
  one – a cat
  creature – the cat

2 Basically, the writer avoids repeating himself by using pronouns, relative pronouns, replacement nouns and possessive adjectives.

2 A rewritten version of *The Princess and the Frog* story

Once upon a time there was a beautiful young princess who happened to be out walking through some woods. Suddenly she saw a frog in a pond. A little distance away she also noticed a large and magnificent castle. At that moment, the small green creature spoke to the young woman. She was quite astonished, not being accustomed to hearing animals speak!

Anyway, everyday she went to the same small pool of water to talk to her new-found friend. Gradually, after many months of this, Esmerelda, for that was her name, discovered that she had fallen in love with the frog.

One day, during one of their regular chats, the frog ventured to ask his beautiful companion for a kiss. Hiding her disgust at the thought, she bent down to do as he asked. At that moment he was suddenly transformed into the most handsome prince Esmerelda had ever had the good fortune to come across. It turned out that a witch had cast a spell on him and taken his castle where she now lived.

Having been released from the spell, the prince went up to the castle and killed his hideous enemy. He then went back to find Esmerelda whom he married shortly after. Needless to say, they lived happily ever after!

© Copyright Longman Group UK Ltd. 1989

Read out versions from different students and discuss in open class any instances where pronoun substitution leads to confusion or lack of clarity.

pp.50–51 LISTENING

If facilities allow, in order to provide an additional communication activity, you could divide the class in half. One half of the class listens to the Cinderella part of the interview and the other half listens to the Dick Whittington part. Students should then be paired up and they should together answer all the questions to both parts – each explaining to the other the answers to the part they did not hear. If you do this, try and get stronger students listening to the Cinderella part, as it is longer.

1 Cinderella

Tapescript
INTERVIEWER: Cinderella is one of the most famous fairy stories in the world, isn't it?
EXPERT: Yes, that's right. In fact, about, there are about 350 versions of the tale have been recorded worldwide.
INTERVIEWER: Presumably, they vary quite a bit.
EXPERT: Oh yes, indeed. In the German version of the tale, for instance, the sisters, well the stepsisters that

is, are, are described as being 'fair of face but ugly in spirit.'

INTERVIEWER: Whereas in the English version they're just plain ugly.

EXPERT: That's right. And in the Italian version of the tale Cinderella only wears rags to cover up her beautiful clothes underneath.

INTERVIEWER: But these are only minor differences, surely?

EXPERT: Well, if you go futher afield, then the story changes quite a lot. In the Indian story help doesn't arrive from a fairy godmother but rather from a magic tree, or rather from a part of it. Which of course we can see in our version in the form of the fairy godmother's wand.

INTERVIEWER: And why do you think the story is so popular?

EXPERT: Well, I think it has to do with the fact that it's a fight between good and evil, it has a happy ending and, perhaps most important of all, it deals with ordinary people.

INTERVIEWER: Just one question before we discuss Dick Whittington. Why is it that Cinderella wears glass slippers?

EXPERT: Ah! Well now. One theory is that the story came into English from the French version of the tale. Now, of course *vert* (V E R T) meaning green and *verre* (V E R R E) meaning glass both have the same pronunciation.

INTERVIEWER: So the translator got a bit mixed up.

EXPERT: Precisely.

INTERVIEWER: Well, let's turn to Dick Whittington, Now, this isn't exactly a fairy story, is it?

Answers

1 False – *there are 350 versions* .
2 True – *they were 'fair of face'*
3 False – *she wears rags over her fine clothes.*
4 True – *there is a magic tree.*
5 False – *the story is popular because it deals with ordinary people.*
6 True – *this could be because **vert** and **verre** sound the same to an English person!*

2 Dick Whittington

Tapescript

INTERVIEWER: Well, let's turn to Dick Whittington. Now, this isn't exactly a fairy story, is it?

EXPERT: No. No, that's correct.

INTERVIEWER: There is some truth in it, then?

EXPERT: Oh yes, there really was a Richard Whittington known as Dick to his friends, but he wasn't born poor and he didn't come up to London to seek his fortune, although he did make a lot of money. He was, in fact, the son of a wealthy knight, Sir William Whittington.

INTERVIEWER: Oh really. But what about the cat? Where does that fit in? A cat can't have made him rich, surely?

EXPERT: Ah, but it did. It's not one of the four-legged variety, though. You see, Whittington made his fortune transporting coal by ship. And, believe it or not, these ships were commonly referred to as cats.

INTERVIEWER: How extraordinary! Is Dick Whittington a story which is only known in Britain ...?

Answers

1 Dick Whittington is not really a fairy story because it deals with someone who existed historically.
2 The real Dick was the son of a wealthy knight. Dick became rich himself.
3 Again, this story revolves around a play on words between French and English. In old French *un echat* was a merchant ship. English people would have only recognized the word *chat* which means cat in English. So Dick, who became rich from trading by ship, became a rich man because of his *cats*! This is one theory of how the story developed.

p.51 READING

This passage, and the listening which comes on the following page, aim to sensitize students as to how present tenses can be used to provide a synopsis of a plot, or tell an anecdote or joke.

1 Answers

1 True
2 True
3 False – *he calls himself Scorpio.*
4 False
5 False – *he kills three people.*
6 False – *three times*
7 False – *Scorpio is freed because of Dirty Harry's methods.*

2 This can be set as homework.

p.52 LISTENING **A tall story**

1 Give students a few minutes to try and make their connections and then encourage them to share their ideas (which can be very amusing) in open class, before listening to the story.

Tapescript

CAROL: I heard this wonderful story the other day which I must tell you.

ARTHUR: Oh my god, not another one of your stories.

CAROL: You're going to hear it anyway so ...

ARTHUR: Go on then, I'm all ears.

CAROL: Well, you see there's this woman and she's driving off to meet a friend in town one day. She's in a bit of a hurry and she doesn't notice the cat asleep in the driveway. Anyway, you can guess what happens next.

ARTHUR: I think I can, yes.

CAROL: She's backing out of the driveway when she hears this little cry as she goes over something.

ARTHUR: The cat.

CAROL: Right first time.

ARTHUR: Go on.

CAROL: Anyway, so she gets out of the car and sees the cat lying there stone dead. And she doesn't know what to do. She's already late for her meeting with her friend and she's thinking 'Where am I going to put Java?'

ARTHUR: What's Java?

CAROL: Oh, Java's the name of the cat. Well, she can't leave it there and she can't put it in the dustbin 'cause the kids might see. Anyway, to cut a long story short, she looks in the car and sees this plastic bag from a rather smart department store.

ARTHUR: I don't believe a word of this.

CAROL: No, it's all true. Cross my heart. So she puts the cat in the bag and drives off to meet her friend. Well, when she's parked the car, she decides to take the bag with her into the department store where she's meeting her friend. You see, she thinks her friend will have some clever idea about what to do with the cat.

ARTHUR: You've got to be kidding!

Carol: No, no. She goes into the shop, oh, and spots a rather nice-looking handbag on the counter and puts down the plastic bag for a sec to have a quick look at it. Can you guess what happens next?

ARTHUR: No. I hate to think.

CAROL: She puts the handbag down and looks for the plastic bag. It's gone, of course. And just then she hears this scream and commotion out in the street. She goes to the door and sees this middle aged woman lying in the street – she'd fainted – with the plastic bag with poor old Java in it beside her on the pavement. You see, she was a shoplifter and, when she'd got outside, she hadn't been able to resist having a peep at what was inside the bag.

ARTHUR: Ridiculous. Still, it makes a good story.

Answers

1B ... *not another one of your stories.*

2C ... *the cat asleep in the driveway.*

3A ... *she can't put it in the dustbin 'cause the kids might see. You see, she thinks her friend will have some clever idea about what to do with the cat.*

4A ... *into the department store where she's meeting her friend.*

5B *she hears this scream ... this middle aged woman ... she'd fainted.*

Extension

In groups of three, get students to choose six items from the following list and make an unusual story based around them which should be as long as possible.

a tin of paint / a lion / a traffic warden / a packet of biscuits / a key / a typewriter / an English teacher / a brick / a piece of string / a tennis ball / a wall / a tractor / an object of your choice

When students have completed their story, put them in new groups where they tell each other the stories they have invented.

pp.52–53 WRITING
The narrative composition

1 Get students to brainstorm what they think they should aim to do in writing a good narrative composition. Put the list on the blackboard and then ask students to read part 1 to compare their ideas with those in the book.

2

1 This composition is good as a result of:
- the wide and appropriate range of structures used.
- the appropriate use of a range of vocabulary and expressions, e.g. *we could hardly believe our luck, needless to say.*
- the choice of certain phrasal verbs, e.g. *held up, pulled up, drove off, found out,* also helps the composition flow nicely.
- the clear and logical organization, with particularly good use of linkers, e.g. *although, when, after, as.*

2 The different past tenses are each used for a particular purpose which students should, by now, be able to analyse fairly confidently. If there are any real problems, refer them back to the explanations at the beginning of the unit.

UNIT 5

A Sense of Adventure

Possible lesson organization

L1	SPEAKING	Choosing a holiday, p.54
	VOCABULARY	p.55
	*USE OF ENGLISH	Allocating holidays, p.55
	READING	A holiday with a difference exs. 1–2, p.56
	Homework	
	WRITING	A holiday with a difference ex. 3, p.56
	USE OF ENGLISH	Dialogue completion, p.58

L2	LISTENING	Talking about a planned holiday, p.57
	PRONUNCIATION	Clear and dark /l/, p.58
	LANGUAGE STUDY	Ways of talking about the future, p.58
	SPEAKING	Role play, p.59
	*USE OF ENGLISH	Question 1 Gap-filling exs 1–3, pp. 59–61
	Homework	
	USE OF ENGLISH	Gap-filling ex.4, p.61

L3	SPEAKING	Discussing texts, p.62
	LANGUAGE STUDY	Obligation and necessity, pp.62–63
	LISTENING	Anita's holiday, p.63
	*WRITING	A letter of complaint exs. 1–2, p.64
	Homework	
	WRITING	A letter of complaint ex. 3, p.64

* These are the items that are most easily done by students at home if classroom time is short.

p.54 SPEAKING
Choosing a holiday

Elicit what is happening in the picture and put all new/important vocabulary on the blackboard. Put students in groups to share their opinions/experiences of the activities in the illustration.

p.55 VOCABULARY

Answers
1 brochure;   2 package tour;   3 safari;
4 souvenirs;   5 charter;   6 resort;   7 half board;
8 self-catering

Extension
Let the students consider the questions in groups:
• Do you like package tours or do you find them restrictive?
• Have you ever been on a safari? Would you like to go on one? Why/Why not?
• Do you generally bring back souvenirs from holidays? If so, what kind of things? What is your most interesting souvenir?
• Have you ever been on a self-catering holiday? If not, would you like to? Do you think it would be too much hard work?

p.55 USE OF ENGLISH

1 Let students read first to say which holiday *they* would prefer and why. Sort out any vocabulary problems at this stage, e.g. *greencoats, sun-soaked, bungalow*. Then put students in small groups to plan their paragraphs for exercise 2 and then give them time to write their answers on their own.

2 Possible answers

> If I were Peter Donaldson, I would go on the Club 20–30 Holiday. Peter enjoys parties and night life and there is a programme with all these activities organized. He doesn't know many people in London and this holiday would be a really good way for him to make friends quickly. Who knows, he might be able to see them when he gets back to London. It's much better than going away on his own.
>
> Albert and Vera Rogers should take the self-catering bungalow advertised in the newspaper. Albert hates hotels and foreign food so they should really stay in a place where they can look after themselves. Vera will be able to play golf and they'll be able to take Sandy the dog for long walks. It would be a peaceful holiday, perfect for elderly people.
>
> If Warren and Diana Harris went to Bontlins, they could have a family holiday within a limited budget. There are special reductions for children and all activities are included in the price so they won't have to worry about any extras. Young couples with children find it difficult to go out on their own but there are baby-sitters at Bontlins and this would let the parents have a good time too.
>
> © Copyright Longman Group UK Ltd. 1989

p.56 READING
A holiday with a difference

1 Having given time for pairs to discuss their most exciting holidays and perhaps had one or two of the most interesting described in open class, ask if anyone has been to West Africa and elicit what students know about the area, e.g. *countries, climate, kinds of crops, what the area is famous for, typical souvenirs.*
On the first read-through students should just concentrate on answering question 1. They check together and then on the second read-through attempt questions 2 and 3.

Answers
1

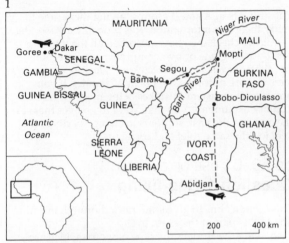

2 Four: train, boat, canoe (pirogues) and taxi
3 Dakar – tie-dyed cloth and jewellery
Abidjan – wood-carving

2 Put students in small groups and nominate a 'secretary' for each group to note down what each group thinks is the correct answer, which part of the text indicates this and *why* the other choices are wrong. Having done this, they should consult the commentary on p.65 and there should be time for open class discussion of any points that students are not happy about.

3 This can be set as homework. You may want to ask one or two students to be prepared to make a presentation to the class of a region they know well and the various places of interest that can be visited.

p.57 LISTENING

1 Students in pairs attempt to name all the objects in the picture first. (You could turn this into a competition to see who could name the most objects.) The objects are: a tent, waterproof clothing (trousers and anorak), rope, a safety helmet, a survival blanket, a map, walking boots, saucepans, a kettle, a camping gas stove, a spoon and fork, a tin opener, a first aid box, a compass and a sleeping bag.

Give students a little time to discuss and decide what *they* think is really necessary to take on a holiday like this. Then listen to the conversation.

Tapescript
FRIEND: What are you doing this summer for your holiday, Julie?
JULIE: I'm going off with some friends. We're going to the Lake District for about ten days or so.
FRIEND: Oh, are you camping?
JULIE: No, we'll be staying in youth hostels most of the time. We're going to do a lot of walking but we'll be able to get to a youth hostel by the end of each day.
FRIEND: Oh, tell me, what will you be taking with you then?
JULIE: Well, a pair of really good walking boots for a start and quite a lot of clothing. You can never be sure what the weather's going to be like. It can be lovely one moment and grotty the next. When you're up high too, it can even snow on a summer's day!
FRIEND: Sounds a bit dangerous. Do you have to take any special equipment or anything with you?
JULIE: No, not really. Oh, we'll take those survival blankets which you can wrap yourself up in, you know, just in case but apart from that nothing special.
FRIEND: Oh yeah, I know. One of those silver things you see them wearing at the ends of marathons.
JULIE: That's it. Oh, a map and compass, of course, sleeping bags for the youth hostel, waterproof jacket and trousers, oh and a camping gas stove and kettle so we can brew up. But no tent. I took one last year but I needn't have bothered. I didn't use it once.
FRIEND: So you've done this sort of thing before.
JULIE: Oh, yeah. This'll be my fourth visit to the Lakes. How about you? Have you got any plans?
FRIEND: Well, I'm not sure. I might be going to Greece or Turkey ...

Answers
– a pair of walking boots
– survival blankets
– a map
– a compass
– sleeping bags
– a waterproof jacket and trousers
– a camping gas stove
– a kettle

2 *I'm going off* with some friends. (present continuous)
We'll be staying in youth hostels. (future continuous)
We're going to do a lot of walking. ('going to' future)
We'll take those survival blankets. (future simple)

31

Note

Students may want to discuss, at this point, the significance of the different forms, in which case you should move straight to the *Language study* section on p.58.

p.58 PRONUNCIATION

Answers

	HOTEL	HOSTEL
1 holiday	✓	
2 tell	✓	
3 able		✓
4 lake	✓	
5 kettle		✓
6 This'll		✓
7 Well	✓	
8 We'll		✓
9 lot	✓	

p.58 LANGUAGE STUDY
Ways of talking about the future

1 Students should work on this in small groups.

Answers
A 6; B 4; C 5; D 1; E 7; F 3; G 2

2 Students should work on this in pairs.

Possible answers
1 Thanks for the invitation, but I'm so tired I'm going to stay at home.
2 Don't cry, darling. I'll buy you another one.
3 I'd love to come out with you but I'm cooking supper for everyone.
4 I will meet you at/ pick you up from the station at seven.
5 Guess what. Sarah's going to have a baby!
6 You'll love the monuments and the parks; you'll hate the weather.
7 You'll get lung cancer if you continue smoking like that.

Extension
Having sorted out *Possible answers* to exercise 2, let students choose *one* situation to expand as a mini-role play. When ready, select some or all to be acted out in front of the class. You may want to give feedback on language points after each role play but remember that use of the appropriate future form is the most important thing.

p.58 USE OF ENGLISH
Dialogue completion

This can be set as homework.

Possible answers
1 What's the cheapest flight you have?
2 How long do you want/ would you like to stay?
3 Will you be spending the weekend there?
4 It costs £70. How does that sound?
5 What times are the flights?
6 Could I have/Could you book me on the 7.30 flight?

p.59 SPEAKING
Role play

Put students in A and B groups, giving them time to study their role information. It is probably a good idea to quickly check they have absorbed all the information by asking one or two comprehension questions, e.g. *What are you doing this weekend? How are you getting there?* before putting students in A/B pairs. If you notice any consistent mistakes being made by a number of students, you may want to go over these at the end and then ask students to change partners (but keeping the same role) and try again.

pp.59–61 USE OF ENGLISH
Question 1 Gap-filling

This section aims to give students a thorough introduction to this part of the exam by:
1 showing the student the type of words which are frequently taken out.
2 providing some intensive practice on those words (in this case, conjunctions, adverbs and determiners), which are taken out.

1 Ask students to quickly read through the text to answer the following questions:
Where did they spend the night? (*on benches*)
Why? (*The cheap hotels were full up.*)
Who do you think 'they' were? (*possibly students as they had little money*)
Then, covering the answers in the left hand column, ask them to quickly try and decide, in pairs, what part of speech each of the words in **bold** is. Then check against the answers.

2

1 For this exercise you may wish to put students in teams and make it a race to see who can finish first.

Answers
A Although; B As; C because; D if; E so;
F Neither; G spite; H Either; I nevertheless;
J however; K while; L during

2 As an introduction to this exercise and to help students where you think they may need it, you may want to write up the following definitions of the target words on the blackboard. Students suggest single words having these meanings **before** looking at the alternatives in the book:
A sufficient;   B in fact;   C almost not;
D surprisingly;   E no more than;   F nearly;
G rather;   H other;   I more than is good;
J completely

Answers
A enough;   B really;   C hardly;   D even;
E only;   F almost;   G quite;   H else;   I too;
J entirely

3 For variety, you may want to do this exercise in the following way: tell students that of the following answers half are correct and half are not. They have to identify the wrong ones and correct them:
A this;   B all;   C little;   D few;   E both;
F which;   G what;   H those

Answers
A this;   B all;   C few;   D little;   E Both;
F what;   G Which;   H those

3 Prior to the exercise, ask students what they know about Marco Polo. Elicit via questions, e.g. *When did he live? What is he famous for?* Read the passage the first time to answer the questions. Read it a second time to decide between the various word choices.

Answers
1 about;   2 already;   3 that;   4 passed;
5 getting; 6 along;   7 Eventually;   8 where;
9 who;   10 by; 11 Although;   12 opportunity;
13 provided;   14 must;   15 down;   16 the;
17 stage;   18 few;   19 captured;   20 During

4 This can be done as homework.

Answers
1 used;   2 whose;   3 the;   4 Although;   5 from;
6 would/could;   7 taken/brought;   8 all;
9 Finally/Eventually;   10 themselves;   11 Anything;
12 under/behind/between;   13 when/after/once;
14 small/little; 15 things;   16 enormous;   17 feel;
18 These;   19 to;   20 on

p.62 SPEAKING
Discussing texts

You may wish to allocate one passage per pair to study and answer the questions before putting students in groups of four where they each explain *their* passage.

Answers
A   1   Someone talking about their holiday
      2   The person who went on the holiday
      3   A conversation between two friends
B   1   Advice is being given to people planning on making a trip to India
      2/3   From the word 'readers' this is clearly a written text, probably a magazine article as the language is quite informal, almost chatty
C   1   On board a plane about to land
      2   The air hostess or steward
      3   As in 1
D   1/2/3   This is a formal text which is from some kind of official form or document. You might read it when applying for a visa.

pp.62–63 LANGUAGE STUDY
Obligation and necessity

1/2 Let students work on exercise 1 in small groups and then put them in pairs to work out the responses for exercise 2 which can be developed into mini-role plays if required.

1 Answers
1 G;   2 E;   3 C;   4 A;   5 D;   6 F;   7 B;   8 H

2 Answers
1 You really must see this exhibition of African art.
2 I have to welcome customers and ask them to check in. I also have to answer the phone and take bookings. I don't have to write letters or anything like that. That's the secretary's job.
3 All students have to do the washing-up when they have eaten their meals. They have to keep quiet after 10.00 and guests have to be out by 11.30.
4 I was going to take a taxi but in the end I didn't have to.
5 I really must pay that bill.
6 When you go to England, you should take plenty of warm clothes.
7 You know all those sandwiches I took? Well, I needn't have taken them with me because lunch was provided.
8 Are you sure I don't have/need to bring any food.

p.63 LISTENING

You may wish to pre-teach the following vocabulary: *strenuous, stuffy, gorgeous, the deck, a pain in the neck, cramped, airy*. Get students to read the questions, play the cassette once, check answers together and then play again. Play through a third time if there are any remaining problems.

Tapescript

FRIEND: Welcome back, Anita. Did you have a good time?

ANITA: Ah, it was great, thanks. I feel so relaxed.

FRIEND: Well, don't worry, it won't last. We've been incredibly busy the last two weeks. But tell me about the holiday. You were on a boat, weren't you?

ANITA: Yes, it was a sailing holiday but the boat had a crew who looked after you and so on. You didn't have to do anything strenuous if you didn't want to.

FRIEND: What were the crew like?

ANITA: Oh, absolutely fantastic. There were half a dozen of them in all. Well, the captain was a real character called Nico. He must've been about 50 and he had this wonderful grey beard. He was tremendous. I've got some photos. I'll bring them in to you when I've got them back.

FRIEND: What about the other people?

ANITA: Oh, they were fine. There was one old girl who was about 70 but she was very lively and then a couple in their early twenties but most of us were in our late thirties, early forties. We all got on really well together, oh, except of course there had to be one complete pain in the neck, Donald, a divorced computer salesman who kept on using all the sailing jargon and being very macho. Oh, he thought he was wonderful. He spent the whole two weeks walking round holding his stomach in. Anyway, I'd rather not go on about Donald.

FRIEND: What were the sleeping arrangements like?

ANITA: Fairly comfortable but the cabins were a bit small and stuffy. It didn't matter, though, 'cause we all slept out on the deck which was marvellous, watching the shooting stars.

FRIEND: Sounds as though you had a lovely time.

ANITA: Oh, I did. The food wasn't that great but the wine was OK and you could have as much as you wanted.

FRIEND: And the men?

ANITA: Well, I met this absolutely gorgeous boy called Savvas. Oh, just like a Greek god he was. Anyway, ...

Answers

1C Nico, Donald, Savvas
2C half a dozen crew, one old girl, a young couple and most (say five or six) in their late thirties, early forties
3C *most of us were in our late thirties, early forties*
4A *the cabins were a bit small*
5B Donald not Ronald

p.64 WRITING
A letter of complaint

1 Let students work on this part in pairs.

Answers

1 He has five complaints:
- accommodation in a modern hotel *not* a small villa
- accommodation in poor condition, e.g. cracks everywhere, walls were paper thin
- only two other young people in the hotel (both men)
- only nightlife was bingo
- rudeness of company representative

2 This is really a matter for discussion between you and the students but examples might be:
I am writing to complain about ...
According to ... was supposed to be ...
To make matters worse ...
On top of everything ...
... I expect ...
I trust you will give this matter your immediate attention.
I look forward to receiving a satisfactory reply by return of post.

3 Reference should be made to the inclusion of the address of the person you are writing to, the particular formulae for opening and closing the letter and the various expressions employed which are specific to more formal letters.

2 Students should compose letters of reply in the same pairs. Then these letters should each be read out with subsequent discussion of particularly good features.

3 This can be set as homework.

UNIT 6

Changes

Possible lesson organization

L1	LISTENING	Rosie's social circles, p.66
	*VOCABULARY	Paper 1, Section A, p.67
	READING	My childhood, pp.68–69
	LANGUAGE STUDY	Different forms of **used to**, p.69

L2	*USE OF ENGLISH	p.70
	LISTENING	Harriet's childhood, p.70
	PRONUNCIATION	Long and short vowels, p.71
	LANGUAGE STUDY	Causative have, p.71
	Homework	
	LANGUAGE STUDY	**make** or **do** in fixed combinations, p.71

L3	WRITING	A biography exs. 1–2, p.72
	*USE OF ENGLISH	Expanding 'dehydrated' letters, pp.73–74
	SPEAKING	Bullying sketch, p.74
	Homework	
	WRITING	A biography ex.3, p.72

* *These are the items that are most easily done by students at home if classroom time is short.*

p.66 LISTENING

1 Students should predict the causes for the changes in the social circles in pairs. Encourage students to use appropriate structures for making deductions, e.g.
*Her grandmother **must have** died.*
*She **might have** lost touch with Simon.*

2 Tapescript

INTERVIEWER: Rosie, you agreed to draw two social circles. Now, would it bother you at all to go into them?

ROSIE: Well, I suppose it could be a bit embarrassing but, well, I'll try and be as straightforward as I can.

INTERVIEWER: I guess the first question that anyone would ask is, what happened to Simon?

ROSIE: I was afraid you'd ask that. Well, to cut a long story short, I'd been going out with him since I was 16. When he was 18, he went away to university and, when he was away, I fell in love with Clive.

INTERVIEWER: Where had you met Clive?

ROSIE: Clive was Simon's best friend from school. I'd known him a long time.

INTERVIEWER: And he'd been going out with Lucy?

ROSIE: Yes, that's right. Well, they split up over something silly and the following weekend there was a party on, and Clive and I went together 'cause Simon was away. Well, it seemed the natural thing to do. Then quite simply we realized we loved each other.

INTERVIEWER: How did Lucy and Simon take this?

ROSIE: Well, Simon was really upset for a while but he soon found a new girlfriend at university. I think he got over it pretty quickly really. As for Lucy, well, she was furious because she said it had only been a lover's quarrel and that I'd pinched Clive off her.

INTERVIEWER: Well, in a way hadn't you?

ROSIE: Yeah, I know it sounds awful and I felt rotten at the time but I couldn't help myself. Later on I made it up with Lucy and we still see each other from time to time.

INTERVIEWER: And what about Simon and Clive?

ROSIE: Well, they fell out completely and haven't spoken to each other since.

INTERVIEWER: And what about your parents? There seems to have been something of a change there.

ROSIE: Well, my dad really liked Simon– he was going off to study to be a doctor and he's quite smart and was always polite – whereas Clive was unemployed at the time and wore an earring and things. Well, there were some terrible rows. Dad even refused to come to the wedding. We're just about talking to each other now but relationships are very tense still. Since Sophie was born, I've been getting on much better with my mum. I get on really well with Tom, my father-in-law, and I've grown much closer to my auntie Cathy.

IITERVIEWER: Why's that?

ROSIE: Well, I was brought up to think of her as the black sheep of the family. She'd been a bit wild when she was young and got kicked out of her home and I think she could understand what I'd been through.

INTERVIEWER: And your grandmother?

ROSIE: Oh, she passed away two years ago.

3 Answers

to fall in love with someone; to split up; to pinch someone off someone else; to get over something; a lover's quarrel; to make it up; to fall out; to get on with someone; to grow closer to someone; to bring someone up; the black sheep of the family; to get kicked out; to pass away

Extension

It may be appropriate for students to draw their own social circles (possibly leaving out any particularly sensitive relationships!) and then explain their significance to a partner, using any relevant vocabulary that came up in the *Listening*.

p.67 VOCABULARY

Give students a time limit of 10 to 15 minutes and let them work on this exercise on their own or in pairs. For students who finish ahead of the others you might ask them to think carefully about why exactly the alternatives they have rejected are wrong.

Answers
1 C; 2 B; 3 A; 4 D; 5 A; 6 C; 7 B; 8 D;
9 C; 10 D; 11 D; 12 C; 13 C; 14 C; 15 C;
16 A; 17 D; 18 C; 19 D; 20 D; 21 C; 22 B;
23 D; 24 D; 25 C

Extension
Having sorted out the correct answers, put students in groups of three to write an exciting and dramatic story using as many of the words in the *Vocabulary* section as possible. Allow about 20 minutes for this, monitoring carefully, helping the different groups as they write. At the end, let each group read out their story, perhaps for fun, noting down the number of target words each group manages to include in their story.

p.68 READING
My childhood

1 As a general introduction to the text, you could ask students to suggest general reasons for problems in family relationships between parents and children, e.g. parents forget what it was like to be young, children don't appreciate why parents can feel anxious.
Possibly pre-teach the following items of vocabulary: *a cot, to look at the world through rose-coloured spectacles, to be insane, tactful, sticking-plaster, to rehearse, fancy-dress.*

Answers
1 She feels positive about it. It seems to have been happy.
2 She had a good relationship with her parents.

2 Put students in groups to work on this. Then put up answers on the blackboard when the class has agreed as a whole – any dissenters must be convinced by reference to the text. At the end give the class a 'mark' and explain any wrong choices and why they were wrong.

Answers
1C *... all the attention moved from me ...*
2B *if ... she would know where we all were ...*
3A *it was only when I reached my late teens that I started to read them ...*
4D *I discussed the subject with my father.*
5B *... blue dress ... a big blue velvet band ... earrings ...*

Extension
You could ask students to relate their own childhood memories in pairs in a parallel fashion to the Maeve Binchy text.

p.69 LANGUAGE STUDY
Different forms of *used to*

1 When students have looked at and attempted to analyse the meaning difference between the examples, make sure they have understood essentially that:
1 *He used to play tennis* conveys the idea that it was a routine in the past but is no longer continued, i.e. he does not play tennis now.
2 *She was not used to living away from home* suggests that this was an activity/state that was unusual for her. She was not accustomed to this situation.
3 *She got used to living away from home* suggests that while, at first, she found it a strange and perhaps difficult situation, after a certain amount of time she adapted to the new way of life. (*Get* in this case means *become*.)

Pronunciation of **used to**
Highlight both the schwa in *to* and the soft s in *used*, the latter being the differentiating factor between: *He is used /s/ to getting up early* and *He used /z/ a hammer to break the window.*

2 Answers
1 No, but it used to be (*a part of Pakistan*).
2 No, they're used to them (*eating with them*).
3 Not really, they're used to it/being criticized.
4 Not any more, but they used to.
5 They should be careful because they're not used to driving on the right.
6 Eventually you get used to them.
7 No, they're used to it. (*the cold*)
8 No, they soon get used to it.

Extension
Put students into pairs and ask them to:
• describe things they used to do but do not do now, because of lack of time, changes of interest.
• discuss if there have been any major changes in their lives recently, e.g. change of job, getting married, having children, changing where they live. If so, have they got used to the new situation yet? What are the most difficult things to get used to?

p.70 USE OF ENGLISH

Exercises 1 and 2 are probably best done as homework with reference to dictionaries.

Answers

1 for; 2 early; 3 these; 4 However;
5 about/just/nearly/only; 6 where; 7 being;
8 which/that; 9 to; 10 the; 11 her; 12 its/the;
13 too; 14 had; 15 except;
16 quickly/immediately; 17 including; 18 own;
19 did/made; 20 was

2 Answers

1 upbringing;   2 youth;   3 childish;   4 childhood;
5 pregnancy;   6 adolescence;   7 adopted;
8 orphanage;   9 retirement;   10 teenage

p.70 LISTENING

Possibly pre-teach:
not to lift a finger
to be spoilt
boarding school
to make a mess of something
to shrink
to be waited on hand and foot
to buy clothes off the peg
Students confer in pairs on the answers to the multiple
choice questions.

Tapescript

HARRIET: As you know, I was born in India. My father
   had a terribly important job – he was in charge of
   building projects for an entire region and supervized
   the construction of dams, roads, bridges and such-
   like. I didn't see much of him as a child as he was
   often away. And when he was home, the house
   would be full of engineers with plans and papers.
   The house I remember very clearly. You wouldn't
   call it a mansion but it was extremely large and
   painted white with a veranda and lovely grounds for
   me to play in. We had servants and all the years we
   were there my mother never had to lift a finger to do
   anything. I had a number of nannies and, being the
   only daughter, I was spoilt by everyone. My two
   elder brothers, poor lambs, were packed off to
   boarding school in England at the age of seven and I
   was brought up with a tremendous sense of my, and
   my family's, self-importance.
   In the summer the women and children would go to
   the hills but the men worked on through the heat on
   the plains. And it was during the summer that my
   father fell ill and could not continue with his job. We
   had to return to England. That was in 1920 and I
   remember being very seasick on the journey home.
   In India everyone talked about going home but the
   reality for me was a terrible shock. When we landed,
   it was cold and grey and I was surprised at seeing so
   many white faces around me. I realized I wasn't
   special anymore. We travelled first class up to
   London but it was nothing compared to travelling
   first class in India. And I was so disappointed in our
   house. It seemed so cramped and dingy. I felt that I
   had really come down in the world. We only had
   one servant and she didn't live in. My mother tried
   to do the cooking – oh, she did her best but at first
   she made a terrible mess of everything.
   But the worst thing about coming back was what
   happened to my father. From being responsible for
   major projects and hundreds of people he suddenly
   became just one of many working in the ministry. He
   never got used to it and somehow seemed to physi-

cally shrink in the last few years before he retired.
As for myself, oh we had always had the best in
India but in England we had to make do with
ordinary things. In India I had my clothes made and
I remember, I am ashamed to say, being terribly
upset at having to buy clothes from a shop, off the
peg as it were. I thought this was awfully common.
And at first I expected to be waited on hand and foot
but gradually I came round to the idea of doing
some of the housework.
Looking back on it, it seems incredible how dramatically my life changed. Actually, I think the change
did me good because my upbringing in India had
made me into such a little snob and coming home to
England taught me what ordinary life was really
like.

Answers

1B *in charge of building projects*
2C *only daughter ... two elder brothers*
3A *the worst thing was what happened to my father*
4D *gradually I came round to the idea of doing some
      of the housework*
5C *I think the change did me good.*

Extension

Summarize the Harriet Williams story changing three
pieces of information – students listen and spot what
they are. The students could then do the same in pairs,
changing different pieces of information.

p.71 PRONUNCIATION
Long and short vowels

Before attempting the discrimination exercise, you may
wish to ask students to look at the tapescript of the
Harriet Williams story (perhaps just the first paragraph) and see how many examples of the target
sounds they can find in the text. They could then listen
to the tape again to check.
e.g.
/ ɪ / = *live, in, India, important, building, bridges*
/ iː / = *region, see, he*

1 Tapescript and Answers

1 reach;   2 feel;   3 pull;   4 fool;   5 shot;   6 cot

2 Tapescript and Answers

1 When did she leave?
2 Was she shot?
3 Can you fill it?
4 He's a little full.
5 What a pretty port!

Extension

Let students, in pairs, try out the discrimination
exercises themselves. Taking it in turns, one to say the
word/sentence, the other to identify which of the
alternatives the first student was attempting to say.

p.71 LANGUAGE STUDY
Causative have

1 Put the two model sentences on the blackboard and give students a little time to try and analyse exactly what the difference is between them. Then they should be directed to the explanation in the Coursebook to compare their ideas.

2 Students should attempt this on their own so that they and you can see any problems that individuals are having.

Answers
1 We had our kitchen redecorated (by a local firm).
2 It's time I had my hair cut.
3 She had her tonsils taken out when she was six.
4 He had his suit altered for the wedding.
5 She had her photographs developed.
6 The woman is having her temperature taken.
7 We had our central heating fixed (by a plumber).
8 Have you had your hair done? You look different.

Extension
As well as suggesting what other things students have done for them, they might like to speculate what certain millionaires or members of royalty have done for them!

p.71 LANGUAGE STUDY
make or *do* in fixed combinations

Answers
make: a mess, the bed, money, an appointment, a fuss, a noise, a fool of oneself
do: nothing, one's duty, someone good, the work, the washing-up

Extension
You may wish to ask students to add any other words/expressions they know which specifically collocate with either *make* or *do*, e.g. *do:* an exercise, homework, the housework
make: a mistake, sense, progress

Note
It should be pointed out to students that there are no rules for when to use *make* and *do* – they just have to learn when they are used.

p.72 WRITING
A biography

1 To introduce the subject, ask who in the class enjoys watching old silent movies. See if students know the names of any of the silent movie stars. They should come up with Charlie Chaplin and, having done so, elicit as much information from the class about him as possible, e.g. what he looked like, style of acting, names of films, any information about his personal life. Then set a time limit for reading the biography and answering the questions.

Answers
1 17 years old; 2 1915; 3 Four films are named; 4 three: England, USA and Switzerland; 5 He was married four times.
2 This exercise does not have exact answers and students need to infer from the information in the text. Whatever answers they decide on should be justified by reference to the text.

	CHILDHOOD	YOUTH	MIDDLE AGE	OLD AGE
happy	1/2	?	3	4
successful	2/3	3	3	2

3 This is best done as homework. You may like to read out a few of the biographies/autobiographies next lesson and let students guess who is being described.
   This may be an area that you could extend into project work, i.e. put students into small groups according to interest in particular famous characters. They would then have up to a week to do the research, after which each group would give a presentation to the rest of the class with, where possible, accompanying pictures, diagrams and slides.

p.73 USE OF ENGLISH

This is the most intensive analysis of this part of the exam in the book.

1 Let students attempt this and discuss their answers together, analysing the types of words that have been omitted. Go through the answer and highlight the frequent omission of:
* auxiliaries, e.g. *am*
* prepositions, e.g. *to*
* pronouns, e.g. *you*
* determiners, e.g. *some*
* conjunctions, e.g. *and*
   and also the need to change tenses, e.g. *see → saw*

2/3 These can either be done as further practice at home or in class.

Answers
Dear Sally,
1 I was delighted to get your letter this morning.
2 I have a very clear memory of Richard. He seems/ed such a nice boy.
3 Congratulations. I hope that you'll be very happy together.
4 Unfortunately I won't be able to come to the wedding.
5 At my age I don't think I would find the journey easy.
6 All the same I would love to give you a wedding present.

7 Will you write and tell me what you would like as a present?
8 My thoughts will be with you both on the big day.
9 Don't forget to send me some photographs and a piece of wedding cake.

Dear Jerry,
1 I am writing to say how sorry I am/was to hear of the death of your grandfather/your grandfather's death.
2 He was such a wonderful man. I will/shall miss him a lot.
3 His sudden death must be/have been a shock to you and your family.
4 I remember having a long conversation with him only a few days ago.
5 He used to be so active in the garden and interested in everything around him.
6 I would really like to attend the funeral and pay my last respects.
7 If it is just a family affair, I will quite understand.
8 Please do not hesitate to contact me if there is anything I can do to help you.

p.74 SPEAKING

To introduce the topic you may briefly want to discuss whether students think that bullying in schools is a serious problem and, if so, what they think can be done about it.

Sample script
A:Dad, Dad!
B:What is it, son?
A:Johnny Smith has been picking on me again.
B:What did he do this time?
A:He took a whole packet of wine gums I'd just bought from the sweet shop.
B:Right, come on, let's go and sort him out. [knock, knock]
C:Yes, can I help you?
B:Listen, your son has been picking on little Brian here and I want a word with him!
C:All right, if you insist. Johnny!
D:Yes, Dad. Something wrong?

Give students a few minutes to prepare. Go round monitoring, helping with language problems as they arise. Then the different groups perform in front of each other.

Revision exercise for Units 4–6

Find and correct the 20 mistakes that appear in the following text. They are all areas of grammar or vocabulary that you have looked at in the last three units.

At the beginning of the Christmas holidays, last year, I had suddenly decided to take a holiday in the sun over Christmas and New Year. Actually, I was just come up with a large sum of money from an old aunt who had imfortunately recently died. So, I went along to the travel agent's and picked up all the different prospectuses what they had telling me about all the different types of holidays available. After looking at them all afternoon I came up with one which sounded perfect and there was a flight the followed day.
In fact, from start to finish quite nothing went right. First of all, while the flight I sat next to an extremely boring young man who insisted on talking to me. Luckily there was a film so I hadn't to put up his conversation for the entirely journey. However, the film was quite good, the food was awful and I was very happy when we were landing at the airport. I was taken to my hotel in a special bus but then when I asked for my key the receptionist said they didn't have a reservation for me and that they only had one room free in the basement with a broken window and no washing facilities. At first I was very angry and did quite a fuss, but eventually I realized I had no choice. I was shown to my room and meanwhile I un-packed I noticed a number of large insects crawled around the walls. I was used to live in hard conditions from days in the army but this was supposed to be a holiday!

Corrected version

At the beginning of the Christmas holidays, last year, I had (1) suddenly decided to take a holiday in the sun over Christmas and New Year. Actually, I was (2) just come up with (3) a large sum of money from an old aunt who had imfortunately (4) recently died. So, I went along to the travel agent's and picked up all the different prospectuses (5) what (6) they had telling me about all the different types of holidays available. After looking at them all afternoon I came into (7) one which sounded perfect and there was a flight the followed (8) day. In fact, from start to finish quite (9) nothing went right. First of all, while (10) the flight I sat next to an extremely boring young man who insisted on talking to me. Luckily there was a film so I hadn't (11) to put up (12) his conversation for the entire (13) journey. However, (14) the film was quite good, the food was awful and I was very happy when we were landing (15) at the airport. I was taken to my hotel in a special bus but then when I asked for my key the receptionist said they didn't have a reservation for me and that they only had one room free in the basement with a broken window and no washing facilities. At first I was very angry and did (16) quite a fuss, but eventually I realized I had no choice. I was shown to my room and meanwhile (17) I unpacked (18) I noticed a number of large insects crawled (19) around the walls. I was used to live (20) in hard conditions from days in the army but this was supposed to be a holiday!

Answers
1. no *had*
2. *had* not *was*
3. *come into* not *come up with*
4. *unfortunately* not *imfortunately*
5. *brochures* not *prospectuses*
6. *which* or *that* not *what*
7. *came across* not *came into*
8. *following* not *followed*
9. *almost* not *quite*
10. *during* not *while*
11. *didn't have* not *hadn't*
12. *with* is missing
13. *entire* not *entirely*
14. *although* not *however*
15. *landed* not *were landing*
16. *made* not *did*
17. *while* not *meanwhile*
18. *was unpacking* not *unpacked*
19. *crawling* not *crawled*
20. *living* not *live*

UNIT 7

The Natural World

Possible lesson organization

L1		
	SPEAKING	Discussing pictures, p.75
	VOCABULARY	p.75
	READING	Greenpeace advert, pp.76–77
	PRONUNCIATION	Saying the **th** sound and **the**, p.78
	*LANGUAGE STUDY	The definite article, pp.78–79
	Homework	
	VOCABULARY	Word building, p.77

L2		
	LISTENING	Dangerous gases, p.77
	VOCABULARY	Phrasal verbs, p.80
	READING	Pollution, pp.80–81
	LANGUAGE STUDY	**make, let** and **allow**, p.81
	*LANGUAGE STUDY	The passive, p.82

L3		
	WRITING	The opinion question, pp.82–83
	SPEAKING	Giving opinions, agreeing and disagreeing, pp.84 + 85
	Homework	
	USE OF ENGLISH	Expanding a letter, p.85

These are the items that are most easily done by students at home if classroom time is short.

p.75 SPEAKING

Once reaction to the photos has been elicited, see if they remind students of any recent events, e.g. Chernobyl, or if they know anything about associated environmental problems, e.g. the Greenhouse Effect.

The four pictures show from the left to right:
1 acid rain destruction of a forest
2 an Alpine scene in autumn
3 fish killed by river pollution
4 a tropical beach

p.75 VOCABULARY

Students should attempt this in pairs. Ask those who finish earlier than the others to mark the stress and think about the correct pronunciation of the target words. Ask students to read each answer out loud to check for correct pronunciation.

Answers
1 environment;   2 pollution;   3 extinct;
4 dumped;   5 acid;
6 reactor, contaminated, fallout;   7 Ecology;
8 waste

p.76 READING
Thank God Someone's Making Waves

1 As an introduction to the text, ask students to cover the text and look at the picture. Let them describe the picture and discuss the meaning of the caption. Ask if the students know what Greenpeace is and if they know of any recent events in which Greenpeace has been involved. Possibly get them to brainstorm different ways in which the environment is currently in danger, if this has not already been done.

Answer
Its aim is to get people to join the pressure group Greenpeace.

2 **Answers**
1 A; 2 D; 3 C; 4 B; 5 B

3 **Answers**
1 assault; 2 wastes; 3 sewage; 4 fumes;
5 plunder; 6 threatened; 7 harness; 8 finite;
9 safeguard; 10 challenge; 11 spearhead;
12 made a stand

Extension
You may want to ask students to discuss:
• how much sympathy they feel towards the ideas expressed in the advertisement.
• how far they feel that Greenpeace and other similar organizations have the right to interfere in the business of individual countries and industries.

p.77 VOCABULARY
Word building

1 You could set this as homework and suggest that students use dictionaries to check their answers.

Answers

ADJECTIVE	NOUN	VERB
wide	width	widen
strong	strength	strengthen
deep	depth	deepen
weak	weakness	weaken
short	shortness	shorten
high	height	heighten

2 Answers

1 deepen; 2 widening; 3 strengthened/deepened;
4 weakness; 5 height

p.77 LISTENING

Ask students if they know anything about any of the
three gases and, in particular, if they know what kind
of dangers they present to the environment.

Tapescript

WHITEHEAD: The Campaign for Clean Air has just
issued a report on air pollution and we have in the
studio Frances Kelly of the CCA who's going to tell
us something about the dangers we face from air
pollutants.

KELLY: Hello.

WHITEHEAD: Let's start with sulphur dioxide which
causes acid rain. I thought the government was
doing something about that.

KELLY: Well, they are, but too slowly. Sulphur dioxide
emissions from power stations are still going on and
the resulting acid rain is still killing off fishes and
plant life in lakes and destroying the forests. And we
in Britain are among the worst culprits when it
comes to this kind of pollution.

WHITEHEAD: What are the other pollutants?

KELLY: Carbon monoxide and carbon dioxide. Carbon
monoxide, which is mostly produced by motor
vehicles can, even in small doses, cause sickness and
a slowing of the reflexes and there is strong evidence
to show that it has an effect on the growth of children.

WHITEHEAD: And carbon dioxide?

KELLY: Well, in a way this is the least dangerous of the
pollutants we've mentioned but in the longer term it
may be the most damaging.

WHITEHEAD: Why?

KELLY: There is clear evidence that the build-up of
carbon dioxide in the atmosphere is the main cause
of the Greenhouse Effect. This will have dreadful
results like the melting of the polar ice caps and
subsequent flooding of low-lying areas.

WHITEHEAD: So what you're saying is that the increased amounts of carbon dioxide in the atmosphere is making it warmer.

KELLY: Yes, that's right and the results will be cata-
strophic.

WHITEHEAD: And what should we be doing about this?

KELLY: Frankly, the government has got to impose far
stricter controls on these emissions and bring in
tough legislation to deal with the problem.

WHITEHEAD: Frances Kelly thank you very much.

KELLY: Thank you.

WHITEHEAD: After the news we hope to be talking to
the Minister for the Environment, Patrick Hilliard ...

Answers

1 sulphur dioxide: *causes acid rain which kills off fishes and plant life in lakes and destroys forests.*

2 carbon monoxide: *mostly produced by cars. Can cause sickness and a slowing of the reflexes. Has an effect on the growth of children.*

3 carbon dioxide: *main cause of Greenhouse Effect which may lead to the melting of the polar ice caps and subsequent flooding of low-lying areas.*

p.78 PRONUNCIATION
Saying the *th* sound and *the*

1 Ways of pronouncing *th*

It is interesting to note Roach's comments on the
teaching of these sounds in *English Phonetics and
Phonology*, (1983), Peter Roach, CUP:
The dental fricatives have sometimes been described as
if the tongue was actually placed between the teeth,
and it is common for teachers to make their students
do this when they are trying to teach them to make this
sound. In fact, however, the tongue is placed *inside* the
teeth ... with the tip touching the inside of the lower
front teeth and the blade touching the inside of the
upper teeth. The air escapes through the gaps between
the tongue and the teeth.

Answers

/θ/	/ð/
throughout	the
earth	breathe
threatened	their
strengthen	this
thin	that
thank	with
	there
	those

Tapescript and Answers

Despite the fact, too, that we can create environmen-
tally-clean industries, harness the power of the sun,
wind and waves for our energy needs and manage the
finite resources of the earth in a way that will safeguard our future and protect all the rich variety of life
forms which share this planet with us.

2 Ways of saying *the*

You may wish to elicit the different pronunciations by
putting the examples [*the sun* and *the earth*] on the
blackboard so that students can analyse the differences
before reading the explanation in the Coursebook.
Having given them a minute to practise the pronunciation of the six examples in pairs, go round the class
quickly checking students' accuracy.

pp.78–79 LANGUAGE STUDY
The definite article

1 Do number 1 in open class as an example and then put students in small groups to attempt both exercises 1 and 2.

Answers
1 C; 2 B; 3 D; 4 I; 5 G; 6 E; 7 A; 8 F;
9 H

2 Answers
1 D; 2 C; 3B; 4 E; 5 A

3 Having sorted out any problems, let students work on this exercise individually before conferring in order to show you and them if they really have got the idea. In going over the answers, make sure students justify their responses with reference to the appropriate rules in exercises 1 and 2, e.g. no. 1: zero article [ex. 2: 1D], definite article [ex. 1: 8F]

Answers
1Ø/the; 2Ø/the; 3 the; 4 a; 5 the /Ø/Ø/Ø/Ø;
6 the; 7Ø/the; 8Ø/the; 9Ø;
10 the/Ø/the/the/the; 11Ø/the/the/a;
12 a/the/the

4 You may choose to set this as homework.

Answers

1 ~~The~~ most people in United States have two cars. *(M above The; the above in)*

2 Mary works in an university. *(a above an)*

3 Did you have the nice time at school today, *(a above the; school crossed)*

Amanda?

4 Beatles are most wonderful group I've ever heard. *(The before Beatles; the before most)*

5 What did you think of book I lent you? *(the before book)*

6 She is going to be doctor. *(a before doctor)*

7 They have two holiday homes, one in mountains *(the before mountains)*
and one at seaside. *(the before seaside)*

8 All people who live in this town work at car factory. *(the before people; the before car)*

9 Where's Mary? She is in sitting room talking on phone. *(the before sitting; the before phone)*

10 She's wearing jeans. In fact they're jeans she *(the before jeans)*

wore last week.

p.80 VOCABULARY
Phrasal verbs

Answers
1 bring this up
2 turns into
3 go ahead with
4 carry on (dumping)
5 turned down
6 die out
7 looking into
8 (shortly) run out
9 get rid of
10 turned up

Extension
After students have worked on this exercise, as further practice you could put them in groups of three or four and give each group member four of the phrasal verbs, each one written on a separate piece of card. Give the group a topic to discuss, e.g. pollution, the aim being for each group member to get rid of his/her phrasal verbs by including them naturally in the conversation. When this is done and the other group members accept that the phrasal verb was used appropriately, naturally and accurately, the student can place his/her card in the middle of the table. The 'winner' is the student who places all his/her cards on the table first. The teacher can be appealed to to arbitrate on any points concerning the accuracy of use of the phrasal verbs. If students particularly enjoy this game, when they have finished, you can give them a new topic and redeal the phrasal verb cards for them to play again.

p.80 READING
Living in the modern world

1 Tell students to put a tick [✓] next to the parts they agree with and a cross [✗] next to the parts they disagree with. Having done this, let them compare their views.

2 Students work on this in pairs, justifying answers from the text.

Answers
1 Not stated
2 True – *... no practical solution.*
3 False – *It is a problem that can be solved ...*
4 Not stated
5 False – the article implies that he chooses not to use his car due to the effect on the environment.
6 True – *... if the public boycotted ... manufacturers would have to change their packaging policies.*
7 True – *What can we do as individuals? ... we should all be prepared to make changes ...*
8 False – *... only by acting as individuals first, can we expect governments to act in their turn.*

3 Answers

1 The first line of each paragraph introduces the topic within it.
2 A *I believe ... In my opinion ...*
  B *Let us begin by ...; the first point I would like to make ...; Furthermore ...; Similarly ...; Let us now look ...; Lastly... Firstly ...; Secondly ...; To sum up ...*
3 *What can be done?*
  What can we do as individuals?

The writer uses questions to allow him to argue his case by going on to answer them.

p.81 LANGUAGE STUDY
make, let and *allow*

1/2 Students read the explanation in 1 before attempting 2. For each of the situations sentences can be made using the following example patterns:
Her father made her stay at home.
She wasn't allowed to go to the disco.
He didn't let her go to the disco.
She was made to stay at home.

p.82 LANGUAGE STUDY
The passive

1 Answers

1 The trees are sprayed each week.
2 More and more pollution is being produced (by that factory).
3 They were seen dumping rubbish.
4 The oil refinery has been broken into by demonstrators.
5 All the evidence had been hidden (by the owners) by the time the police arrived.
6 The reactor was being redesigned (by a scientist).
7 The problem can be understood by a child.
8 The enquiry is going to be opened by the prime minister.
9 The police shall be notified about this matter.
10 The newspapers should have been written to.

2 Answers

1 present simple: object + *am/is/are* + past participle [see ex.1:1 above]
  past simple: object + *was/were* + past participle [see ex.1:3 above]
2 present continuous: object + *am/is/are* + *being* + past participle [see ex.1:2 above]
  past continuous: object + *was/were* + *being* + past participle [see ex.1:6 above]
3 'going to' future: object + *am/is/are* + *going to be* + past participle [see ex.1:8 above]
4 present perfect: object + *has/have* + *been* + past participle [see ex.1:4 above]
  past perfect: object + *had* + *been* + past participle [see ex1:5 above]

5 modals like *'can'* and *'must'*: object + modal + *past participle be* + [see ex.1:7 above]
6 modals in the past: object + modal + *have been* + past participle [see ex.1:10 above]

Extension
As further practice of the passive within the topic of the unit, you may like to ask students to prepare a three minute programme aimed at persuading people to join Greenpeace, to be recorded either on cassette or video. It would draw on many of the ideas already presented in the unit. The following are examples of the type of language that might be included:
*As we all know the earth **is being** slowly **poisoned** ...*
*Large areas of rain forest **have been cut down** ...*
*In the years to come, unless something is done, the ozone layer **will be destroyed** ...*

p.82–83 WRITING
The opinion question

1 Explain that there is usually one discursive composition in Paper 2 and ask students to suggest what they think success depends upon in answering this question. Put all ideas on the blackboard and then let them read 1 in the Coursebook to compare their ideas and possibly discuss differences or additional points.

2 Vocabulary

Let students answer this in pairs and then have the answers read out to check on good pronunciation, particularly of target vocabulary.

Answers
1 G; 2 D; 3 I; 4 C; 5 B; 6 A; 7 E; 8 F; 9 H

3 Reading

When the students have matched the pictures to the paragraphs, tell them to look through the text again and highlight any parts that they think they might find useful to them in their composition.

Answers
1 Stop using money against the poor
2 Aim for social justice
3 Give back the land
4 Control the corporations
5 Put food first

4 Discuss in open class:

- the dangers of not doing a plan, e.g. writing incoherently, going off the point, suddenly deciding you should have started in a different way
- how long should be spent on a plan – for a 45 minute composition approximately 10 minutes

- the different ways of making a plan, e.g. the traditional linear fashion with an idea of what will go in each paragraph or a mind-map
- the different things that need to go in a plan for this particular composition, e.g. introduction to problem, various solutions to the problem plus arguments for and against each one, conclusion, including writer's view of the way forward

Pairs plan the composition which could either be written up for homework or done in class with a time limit of approximately 35 minutes. Don't forget to refer students to the useful language and stylistic devices they noted in the *Pollution* article.

p.84–85 SPEAKING
Giving opinions, agreeing and disagreeing

1 Before letting students look at the table of exponents in their books, write an opinion on the blackboard, e.g. *English food is the best in the world!*

Elicit from students that this is an opinion and not a fact! Get them to suggest varying ways of introducing such an opinion. Put all appropriate suggestions on the blackboard and make sure that all the exponents in the book are included. Ask students which words would most naturally be stressed in each case. Go round the class getting students to repeat the model opinion as enthusiastically as possible using a different exponent each time. When students can do this accurately, give prompts of subjects where opinions can easily be expressed – these will vary depending on the local context and the interests of your particular students but subjects might include *smoking, football* and *people who drink and drive.*
After this, elicit ways of agreeing and disagreeing with the model sentence. Again, try and include all the exponents that are referred to in the book. Put them on the blackboard and make sure that students can pronounce them accurately. Then give opinions about any of the subjects that have already come up and get students to agree or disagree with you depending on their real views. This should provide adequate practice before students do exercise 2.

2 One way to do this exercise would be to write the various statements on pieces of paper and put them on walls in different parts of the classroom. Half the students go and stand by a statement they agree/disagree with. The other half move around challenging their opinions.

3 Role play
Explain the general situation and then let students read the introductory text. Ask one or two comprehension check questions to make sure everyone has got the idea. Then allocate each student a role and put all students with the same role together. Let them read through their role cards and help each other with any problems. Go round each group checking everything has been understood, helping with any problematic vocabulary. Particularly check that the Mr/Mrs Dobsons realize what is involved in chairing a meeting. (They will also be responsible for ensuring decisions are made and reporting these back to the rest of the class at the end of the meeting.) Students should then, still in the same groups, discuss what arguments they are going to use in the meeting and what language they think might be useful. Having allowed adequate time for preparation, put students in groups for the actual meeting and let them begin. Set a time limit for the meeting and at the end ask each Mr/Mrs Dobson to summarize the decisions their group made.

p.85 USE OF ENGLISH

This can be set for homework.

Answers
1 I am writing to complain about the dirt and smoke which comes/coming from your factory chimneys.
2 Two days ago I decided to do my washing.
3 I washed the sheets and put them out to dry as it was a nice sunny day and there was a breeze.
4 When I took the washing in, I was horrified to discover that it was covered in dirty marks.
5 I assume that the breeze I mentioned carried/must have carried the dirt from your chimneys.
6 If this is the case, I must complain in the strongest possible terms.
7 This is not only because of my sheets but (also) because we have two small children who are made to breathe the same air.
8 Until this incident I thought your chimneys were safe and clean.
9 I have already written to the/my/our local Member of Parliament about this matter.
10 Furthermore, I must warn you that I am going to write to the local newspaper tomorrow.
11 I look forward to receiving your reply.

UNIT 8

Judging by appearances

Possible lesson organization

L1	SPEAKING	Deducing character from photos, p.86
	READING	Secrets of the face, pp.86–87
	LANGUAGE STUDY	Predictions and guesses, p.88
	PRONUNCIATION	/æ/ /ʌ/ /ɑː/, p.89
	VOCABULARY	Adjectives of personality, pp.90–91
	Homework	
	LANGUAGE STUDY	A further passive construction, p.89

L2	VOCABULARY	Physical description and adjective order, pp.92–93
	LISTENING	Missing person news item, p.94
	SPEAKING	Problem-solving, p.94

L3	LISTENING	Lonely hearts, p.95
	VOCABULARY	Word building, p.96
	*USE OF ENGLISH	p.96
	*SPEAKING	Describing a photograph, p.97

* These are the items that are most easily done by students at home if classroom time is short.

p.86 SPEAKING

Introduce the topic generally by asking the class what they think you can tell about a person's character from their face. Then put them in small groups to look at the photographs. Give them a few minutes and then get feedback from each group.

Photos
A Ronnie Biggs – one of the Great Train Robbers who is in Brazil
B Raisa Gorbachev
C Chris Bonington – Britain's most famous mountaineer
D Jerry Hall – fashion model married to Rolling Stone Mick Jagger
E Frank Bruno – British boxer
F Claire Rayner – agony aunt who gives advice on people's personal problems

pp.86–87 READING
Secrets of the face

1 Elicit questions from the class and put them on the blackboard. Then ask students to read the text as quickly as possible just to find the answers to these questions, if they are in the text.

2 Check that students understand the vocabulary in the questions before they read the text again. As usual, they should be able to justify their answers by reference to the text.

Answers
1A ...*consisted of jealously guarded secrets* ...
2C ... *men with flat noses ... will make ... rather dull husbands.*
3B ... *one which is diamond shaped is a jade-face.*
4A ... *people with eyes of different sizes are often brought up by stepparents.*
5A the implication of paragraphs 4 and 5

4 Remind students of the language of giving opinions, agreeing and disagreeing which they studied in the last unit and which they may find useful during their discussion.

p.88 LANGUAGE STUDY
Predictions and guesses

1
Answers
1C; 2E; 3A; 4D; 5B

2
Answers
1 These secrets *cannot have been* that well guarded.
2 ... men with flat noses ... *will* make shy ... husbands.
3 ... she *must be* strong-willed ...
4 ... this time *must have been* a period of great unhappiness.

Note
At this stage you may decide to do the *Pronunciation* section on p.89 which looks at these modals in particular.

3 You might like to remind students of ways of making their predictions sound less certain, e.g. *I will* **probably** *be married in ten years' time, I* **might** *have some children and I* **certainly hope** *I'll have a better job!*

4 Go through the various pictures in open class, first eliciting descriptions of each, providing vocabulary as necessary. Then put students in pairs to make appropriate deductions.

Possible answers
1 He must have been in a fight.
2 She might have had a row with her boyfriend.

3 She must have been somewhere sunny on holiday.
4 He must have broken his leg skiing.

Note
If you do the *Pronunciation* section after exercise 2, then insist on accurate production of the target items here.

Extension
Topics for further, freer practice of this area include speculation on:
• how the Pyramids/Stonehenge were/was built
• what happened to the crew of the *Marie Celeste*
• any recent local unsolved mystery that has come up in the news

p.89 PRONUNCIATION

Some students may have learnt the American pronunciation of *can't*, approximating to /cænt/. As part of the whole question of what is 'correct' English, we would recommend that you teach those forms of English pronunciation, vocabulary (and grammar) which are most natural to you, whilst at the same time making students aware of alternative forms, particularly as in Papers 4 and 5 of the exam students may be faced with a range of accent. As far as students individually are concerned, perhaps the most important thing is that they are **consistent** in the form of English they produce and do not mix, for example, American and English vocabulary and pronunciation.

1 Answers

can	must	can't
cat	cut	cart
ham	hum	harm
match	much	march
hat	hut	heart

2 Tapescript and Answers

1 cut; 2 harm; 3 match; 4 march; 5 hut;
6 hat; 7 hum; 8 much; 9 cat; 10 ham;
11 heart; 12 cart

Note
If students find this exercise difficult, you could go back and model some of the target words again but only asking students to try and discriminate between **two** of the sound columns at a time. Once students can do this successfully, go back and let them try and discriminate between sounds across all three columns.

3 Make sure the vocabulary is understood before starting the exercise, especially *stuff, staff, batter, soap*. Also, note that *can* in A and F could also be naturally pronounced with the schwa /ə/.

p.89 LANGUAGE STUDY
A further passive construction

This can be set as homework.

Answers
1 The Mona Lisa is claimed to be the world's most famous painting.
2 It is believed to have been a portrait of a nobleman.
3 Her smile is said to hide a secret.
4 It is believed to be Leonardo's masterpiece.
5 He is known to have been a wonderful engineer too.
6 He is thought to have been unhappy in old age.

pp.90–91 VOCABULARY
Adjectives of personality

1 Let students look at the words in the box before they start the exercise. In small groups they should try and think of a synonym or simple explanation for each one. Open class feedback: if one group doesn't know a word, let another group explain it. If no one knows a word, then give a brief definition with example. Then let the students in the same group work through the exercise and this should establish whether they really have understood the meaning of the target vocabulary. Monitor correct pronunciation of target vocabulary carefully. Beware of the words that may act as 'false friends' to speakers of Latinate languages, e.g. *sensitive, sensible, sympathetic*.

Answers for exercises 1 and 2

	ADJECTIVES	NOUNS
1	reliable	reliability
2	sensitive	sensitivity
3	mean	meanness
4	strict	strictness
5	cheerful	cheerfulness
6	sensible	sense
7	nice	niceness
8	sympathetic	sympathy
9	tough	toughness
10	clumsy	clumsiness
11	silly	silliness
12	shy	shyness
13	selfish	selfishness
14	trustworthy	trustworthiness
15	gentle	gentleness
16	bad-tempered	bad temper
17	loyal	loyalty
18	dull	dullness
19	stubborn	stubbornness
20	crafty	craftiness

Extension
In small groups students discuss what they think are the three characteristics they most like/dislike in other people.

3 Check that students know the vocabulary of the descriptions before starting the exercise.

pp.92 – 93 VOCABULARY

Physical description and adjective order

3 Height and build

Answers

1 *tallish, shortish, youngish* ... essentially, all short adjectives

2

	frail	(old) and weak-looking.
	stocky	shortish but well-built.
Someone who is	slim	is attractively thin.
	plump	overweight.
	skinny	unattractively thin.

3 *From left to right*: plump, stocky, skinny, slim, frail

3 Age

Answers

A 65 plus;   B 13 – 19;   C 17 – 20;
D someone who has retired from work, 60 – 65 plus;
E 40 – 55;   F 2 – 3;
G 31 – 33 (*early*), 34 – 36 (*mid*), 37 – 39 (*late*)

5 Answers

Susan has got large round brown eyes.
Klaus has got small bright blue eyes.
Mary has large green eyes.
Mariko has large almond-shaped dark brown eyes.

6 Answers

1 B; 2 A; 3 F; 4 E; 5 D; 6 C

7 Answers

1D; 2E; 3A; 4C; 5B

8 This could be followed up by students writing about someone they know well both in terms of personality and physical description.

p.94 SPEAKING

Ask students to quickly read through the information first to check if they remember all the vocabulary. If they don't, let other students explain it to them.

Solution

NUMBER NAME	1 Emily	2 Charles	3 Anna	4 Diana	5 Brian
AGE	late 30's	middle-aged	elderly	middle-aged	young
BUILD	plump	skinny	slim/skinny	rather overweight	stocky
HAIR	curly brown	bald	straight	straight	wavy
COMPLEXION		pale			
EXTRA FEATURES	freckles	moustache	wrinkles, glasses	limp	beard

Groups who finish early should divide up and go and help out other groups who are having problems.

p.94 LISTENING

Tapescript

NEWSREADER: Police have stepped up their hunt for eight-year-old Neil Graham who's been missing since Friday when he left St. Mark's Primary School to walk home. Neil was wearing jeans, a dark blue pullover and a red anorak and was carrying a yellow satchel. The police have issued a description of a man they would like to interview. The man, who was seen in Castle Street getting into a yellow Renault 5 with a child answering Neil's description shortly before half past four on Friday, is described as being in his early forties, white, balding and of medium height and wearing a leather jacket, jeans and metal-framed spectacles. Police are appealing to anyone with information to come forward.

Answers

1
A True
B Not stated
C False – not *probably* and *satchel* not *bag*
D True
E False – not *may have been*
F False – *shortly before half past four*

---

age: *Early forties*   height: *medium*
hair: *balding*   glasses: *metal-framed*
dress: *leather jacket and jeans*
car: *yellow Renault 5*
any other details: *white*

_____

---

p.95 LISTENING

1 Before looking at the book, set the scene by discussing what lonely hearts columns are and where you might find them. Ask students if they exist in their countries and, if so, if they read them. Ask what they think of them. Then go through the descriptions in the column in the book. Ask students to choose the ad they would be most interested in answering! Sort out any problematic vocabulary as it comes up.

2 Tapescript

CLIVE: Hi, Jenny.
JENNY: Hi.
CLIVE: How did it go, then?
JENNY: Pretty mixed, really.
CLIVE: Oh yeah.
JENNY: Yeah, he wasn't exactly the man of my dreams.
CLIVE: What happened then?
JENNY: It was pretty nerve-wracking, actually, waiting outside the station for him to turn up. Like being 14 all over again.
CLIVE: Yes, I know what you mean. Still, he didn't stand you up, did he?
JENNY: No, no. He turned up all right.
CLIVE: So what did he look like?
JENNY: Well, he had reddish hair, glasses – quite good-looking, I suppose, not very tall, about your height, in fact.
CLIVE: Charming!
JENNY: I didn't mean it like that but I guess I was expecting someone much sportier, someone who likes the outdoor life.
CLIVE: Well-dressed?
JENNY: Not particularly. Bit scruffy, really. Wore a leather jacket and a pullover.
CLIVE: Really?
JENNY: Yeah.
CLIVE: And what was he like?
JENNY: Not that exciting, I'm afraid.
CLIVE: Why not?
JENNY: Well, at first I thought he was OK but then we went off to a pub and all he could talk about was politics.
CLIVE: But you're into that, aren't you?
JENNY: Yeah, but not *all* the time. He went on and on. He said he had a great time but I couldn't get away fast enough.
CLIVE: Oh dear.
JENNY: He wants to see me again. Asked me if I wanted to go to a demo on Saturday.
CLIVE: You're kidding.
JENNY: No. I'm not going. Anyway, how about you?
CLIVE: Well, I have to admit that I almost chickened out.
JENNY: Typical.
CLIVE: Well, I didn't and I had a great time.
JENNY: Did you? Tell us all about it then.
CLIVE: We just went out to an Italian I know and had a nice meal and chatted away merrily. You know, we found out that we'd lived in the same street as kids.
JENNY: How amazing!
CLIVE: But we couldn't remember each other.
JENNY: Was she pretty?
CLIVE: Very. She was very chic – all in black, short black hair and not much make-up.
JENNY: She sounds a bit serious to me. Not really your type.
CLIVE: No, no, not at all. She had a great sense of humour. Funny, you don't expect that from someone who's an accountant.

JENNY: Going to see her again?
CLIVE: Yeah, she said to give her a call.

Answers
Jenny – FRIENDLY, leftish man ...
I was expecting someone who likes the outdoor life. (walks)
... all he could talk about was politics. (leftish)
Clive – BRIGHT, professional woman ...
She had a great sense of humour. (bright, happy)
an accountant (professional)

3 Answers

Jenny – C ... *glasses ... wore a leather jacket and pullover.*
Clive – 4 *all in black ... short black hair and not much make-up.*

4

As an extension to *Discussion point 2*, you could ask students to write their own advertisement for a lonely hearts column. When everyone, including you!, has done this, collect them all and read them out one by one, asking the class to guess who wrote each one. (This should be kept on a fairly light-hearted level!)

p.96 VOCABULARY
Word building

1 Answers

ADJECTIVE	OPPOSITE	ADVERB	NOUN
happy	unhappy	happily	happiness
sympathetic	unsympathetic	sympathetically	sympathy
reliable	unreliable	reliably	reliability
kind	unkind	kindly	kindness
loyal	disloyal	loyally	loyalty
honest	dishonest	honestly	honesty
patient	impatient	patiently	patience
responsible	irresponsible	responsibly	responsibility
sensitive	insensitive	sensitively	sensitivity

2
un; dis; im; ir; in

p.96 USE OF ENGLISH

1
Do the example in the book on the blackboard and then elicit the explanation from the students.

2
Let students attempt this individually before checking together.

Answers
1 irresponsible;   2 sensitivity;   3 unkindness;
4 enjoyably;   5 Luckily;   6 stubbornness;
7 misery; 8 unreliability;   9 ambitious;   10 tactless

Describing a photograph

1 Ask students to just look at the photo first and elicit a full description, possibly by asking each student to contribute one sentence. This should all be done with the gapped text covered. Having done this, they should complete the text.

Answers
1 shows; 2 would say; 3 It looks as though; 4 tell; 5 the background; 6 looks; 7 could be; 8 Perhaps; 9 looks like; 10 can't be; 11 takes after; 12 she has got; 13 make it out; 14 might; 15 maybe

2
1 We use an adjective after *look* when it means *seem*, e.g. *She looks fed up.*
2 *look like* basically means *be similar to*, e.g. *She really looks like her mother.*
3 *look as though/if* has a meaning similar to 1 but attention must be paid to the grammatical construction, i.e. *look + as if/though + subject + verb*, e.g. *The mother looks as though she is in her late 20s.* Note that *as if* and *as though* are interchangeable.

UNIT 9

Teenage Cults

Possible lesson organization

L1	SPEAKING	Picture story, p.98
	VOCABULARY	Clothes, p.99
	LISTENING	Buying clothes, p.99
	SPEAKING	Fashion discussion, p.99
	PRONUNCIATION	Rising intonation, p.100
	*READING	Understanding teenage cults, pp.100–101
	Homework	
	LANGUAGE STUDY	Conjunctions, p.102
	VOCABULARY	Phrasal verbs, pp.102–103

L2	READING	A letter to an agony aunt, p.103
	USE OF ENGLISH	p.104
	VOCABULARY	Participle adjectives, p.105
	*LANGUAGE STUDY	Reported speech exs. 1–5, pp.106–107
	Homework	
	WRITING	Advice letter composition, p.105

L3	LANGUAGE STUDY	Reported speech ex. 6, p.107
	LISTENING	A radio phone-in, p.108
	WRITING	exs. 1–3, pp.108–110
	*USE OF ENGLISH	exs. 1, 2 and discussion of exercise 3, pp.110–111
	Homework	
	USE OF ENGLISH	Written answer to ex. 3

* These items are the ones that are most easily done at home by students if classroom time is short.

p.98 SPEAKING

To begin with, put the students into pairs or groups. They should tell the story using narrative tenses. Then get feedback to the story.

Possible version

1 One morning the Harrison family were having breakfast at the start of another typical day.
2 Liz left for school, saying goodbye to her mum.

3 Unbeknown to her parents, Liz had arranged to see Pete, a good-looking guy she had met at a party the weekend before. She took a new outfit with her in a plastic bag. She showed it to her school friends at the bus stop.
4 Instead of going to school, Liz went into a Ladies to change and get ready for her date.
5 A little while later she made her way over to the park where she had agreed to meet Pete.
He thought she looked wonderful and they walked around the park for the next couple of hours, chatting. They both liked each other a lot. Eventually Liz said she had to go. They agreed to walk home via Pete's house which was closest.
6 As they were saying goodbye outside Pete's house, Liz's dad drove past and saw them. He was very surprised and quite angry.
7 When Liz finally got home, her dad confronted her angrily as she was going up the stairs to her room. Liz ran up to her room, crying.
8 Liz's gran, who was staying with them for a few days, saw what happened and, afterwards, went into the living room to have a word with her son. She reminded him of one or two similar episodes in *his* teens which made him think he had been a little hard on Liz.
9 He went upstairs and apologized for being so angry.

Now encourage the students to work out what was actually said in each of the bubbles. Accept what is best and establish a 'standard' version. You will then be able to refer back to this when you have revised reported speech.

Possible version

What the people might have said/thought:

2	LIZ:	Bye, Mum.
	MUM:	Bye, Liz.
3	LIZ:	So ... what do you think of it?
	FRIEND:	Not bad. Where did you get it?
	FRIEND 2:	I think it's great ... just what you need!
6	DAD:	I can't believe my eyes! Is that ... LIZ?!!
7	DAD:	What do you think you were doing with that boy in the middle of Park Street?
	LIZ:	We weren't doing anything wrong!
8	DAD:	I remember being a bit of a tearaway on that old Triumph bike.
9	DAD:	I'm sorry. I shouldn't have got so angry ... it's just I'm worried about you.
	LIZ:	I know Dad – it's all right, but really, there's nothing to worry about.

Extension

Students may like to discuss who they feel most sympathy for in this situation and why?

p.99 VOCABULARY
Clothes

Answers

1 tight;   2 shrink;   3 match;   4 wardrobe;   5 suits;
6 baggy;   7 loose;   8 clash;   9 take ... in, up;   10 go

p.99 LISTENING

Tapescript

1

CUSTOMER: Yes, these jeans are a really good fit. I'll take 'em.

SHOP ASSISTANT: And what about the dungarees?

CUSTOMER: The dungarees? I think I'll leave them. They don't really suit me. They make me look enormous.

2

CUSTOMER: Oh, these trousers are fine but they're a little too long in the leg.

SHOP ASSISTANT: Well, they are a bit on the long side but we can always get them turned up for you.

CUSTOMER: I suppose that costs extra.

SHOP ASSISTANT: I'm afraid so, sir. They have to go to an outside tailor and the charge is £7.50.

CUSTOMER: £7.50! That's outrageous. I don't think I'll bother with them at all.

SHOP ASSISTANT: And the shirt?

CUSTOMER: Oh yeah, I'll take that. You accept Visa, don't you?

SHOP ASSISTANT: Yes.

3

CUSTOMER: What do you think, Carol?

CAROL: Well, to tell you the truth, I don't think it goes with the top at all.

CUSTOMER: It does clash a bit but I think it'll be all right with some of my other blouses. The only thing is it's a bit loose.

CAROL: A bit loose! It could hardly be much tighter.

CUSTOMER: I think I'll take it but I'll leave the top. I can't afford both.

Answers

	CUSTOMER 1	CUSTOMER 2	CUSTOMER 3
What did they buy? What didn't they buy? Why not?	jeans dungarees make me look enormous	shirt trousers the cost of getting them turned up	a skirt the top can't afford both

Extension

Allocate one of the shop situations from the *Listening* to each pair of students. They should then try acting it out – point out that they should not try and replay the original scene word by word but improvize, just getting across the general content.

p.99 SPEAKING

Let students discuss the points in their groups and then get feedback in open class at the end. You may also like students to predict what they think future fashions will be like.

p.100 PRONUNCIATION
Rising intonation

Answers

1 A *The dungarees?* – indicates the customer had temporarily forgotten about them
  B *£7.50!* – indicates shock at the price
  C *A bit loose!* – indicates surprise at (and disagreement with) this view

2 **Possible stimuli and responses**
A I'm going to marry my teacher. Marry your teacher!
B I had an accident on the way to school. An accident! Are you OK
C I knocked over a cyclist. A cyclist! Was she hurt?
D I'm going to give up English and study Russian. Russian!
E I took some money from your wallet. From my wallet. Why didn't you ask?
F I can't pay you back until the end of the month. The end of the month!

Extension

When students have had time to try acting out these situations, allocate one of them to each pair of students for them to try acting out again but this time also adding and improvizing the time before the showing of surprise and the time after.

p.100–101 READING
Understanding Teenage Cults

1 Pre-teach: *a cult, eye shadow, to look down on someone.* After students have quickly read the article, ask them to say which explanations they find least and most convincing and to say why.

2 **Answers**

1B *The main influence on teenagers remains their friends.*
2C implication of the whole paragraph
3D *Even ordinary society has its drugs.*
4A *There seems to be a lot of truth in this.*
5C *... most kids want to be something and cults give them something to be.*

3 After students have made notes in small groups, they should stand up and move round the classroom finding out what other students know and, where appropriate, adding to their notes. Monitor and help out with vocabulary as the need arises.

Notes

Hippies: Originally from California. 1960s. Bright 'psychedelic' clothes and long hair. Like rock and folk music with a message. Anti-materialistic believing in peace and (free) love. Basically optimistic. Mostly well-off middle class kids reacting against their parents.

Many university students. Usually left-wing and into peaceful demonstrations.

Punks: 1970s .Wear black leather, cut jeans. Brightly dyed hair with spiky or Mohican style haircuts. Like violent discordant music. Anti-materialistic from necessity as they usually come from poor backgrounds. Pessimists.

Skinheads: Wear jeans, ex-army clothing and big boots. They enjoy fighting. They like similar music to the punks. They are often poorly educated and come from working class backgrounds. Frequently right wing and racist.

p.102 LANGUAGE STUDY
Conjunctions

Answers
1 C;   2 B;   3 B;   4 C;   5 B;   6 C;   7 C;   8 A;
9 B; 10 A

pp.102–103 VOCABULARY
Phrasal verbs

1 Answers
1 E;   2 F;   3 H;   4 B;   5 I;   6 G;   7 C;   8 A;
9 D

2 Answers
1 faced up to;   2 let ... down;   3 live up to;
4 look up to;   5 put ... down;   6 look down;
7 talking ... over;   8 go along with;   9 sort ... out

p.103 READING
Having established what the problem is, put students in groups to come up with appropriate advice. Open class feedback.

p.104 USE OF ENGLISH
1 Firstly get students to quickly skim the text to compare Angela's advice with what they came up with. Was it the same? If different, what do they think of Angela's advice? Next, put students in pairs to make the necessary changes/additions to the text.

Answers
1 I think you should follow your husband's example and try to put this incident behind you and your family.
2 Your daughter knows she has let you down and will not feel happy until she feels you have forgiven her.
3 Your feelings of guilt are unjustified and you should put your energy into making your child feel better.
4 If I were you, I wouldn't worry too much about her turning to crime.
5 She has been terrified by the whole thing and has been put off ever taking anything again.

6 Most kids do something like this at some stage and she was just unlucky enough to be caught.
7 If she doesn't get over the experience soon, you can always take her away on a short holiday and give her a change of scene.
8 Then she can face up to her relatives and neighbours.
9 I am sure that you can sort things out.

Note
Highlight those parts of the various expressions in the text used for giving advice, e.g. *I think you should* and *If I were you.* Ask students if they know any other exponents.

2 Students read through the letter quickly and summarize the problem in pairs. They then complete the task.

Answers
1 used/had;   2 on/along;   3 his;   4 really;
5 had; 6 would/could;   7 already;   8 time;   9 as;
10 accused;   11 so;   12 knew/realized/understood;
13 taken/stolen;   14 Since;   15 what;   16 want;
17 all/both;   18 the;   19 for;   20 this

Note
Students should discuss possible advice before attempting the composition in the next section.

p.105 WRITING
This can be set as homework.

p.105 VOCABULARY
Participle adjectives

1 Put *I'm bored!* and *I'm boring!* on the blackboard. Ask students to analyse and explain the difference in meaning. They should then read 1.

2 Answers
1 horrified;   2 depressed;   3 disappointing;
4 worrying;   5 disgusting;   6 tiring;   7 boring;
8 boring

pp.106–107 LANGUAGE STUDY
Reported speech

1 Corrected sentences
1 He said the problem was difficult.
   or He told me the problem was difficult.
2 She told him to turn down the music.
3 He asked her how much money he had taken.
4 He asked whether he could help.
5 She explained the problem to him.

2 Tense changes

2 Mary: I'm working.
present continuous
3 She said she had been to Spain.
past perfect
4 I've been living here for ages.
present perfect continuous
5 She told me she had made a mistake.
past perfect – no change
6 She said she had been watching TV.
past perfect continuous

3 Changes with modals

1 *may, can* and *will* usually become *might, could* and *would*.
2 Generally there is no change but note that if we use the perfect infinitive (*have* + past participle) then we invariably change our intended meaning, e.g. *I should post this letter.*
→ He said he should post the letter. (reminding himself)
→ He said he should have posted the letter. (He didn't.)
3 She told him if he did that again, she would hit him.

4 Other changes

1
A 'I'm going to leave tomorrow,' she said.
B 'This is the record I bought two days ago,' he said.
C 'The parcel will arrive the day after tomorrow,' they said.
D 'Did anybody come yesterday?' he asked.
E 'Your flat will be ready next month,' we told them.
F 'I called this morning but no one answered the door' he said.
G 'Is today your birthday?' she asked.

2 REPORTED SPEECH
A that
B the
C that day
D the day before/the previous day
E two days before/earlier
F earlier
G the following/next day
H in two days' time
I the following week/month/year

5 Reporting advice and suggestions

Possible answers
A She advised him to go by train.
B Arthur suggested watching TV.
C Julian suggested that she should go to the cinema.
D The doctor advised her to take more exercise.
E Fatima's grandmother advised her to wear a scarf.

6 Answers

1 Carol told Peter not to make so much noise.
2 Sue advised Richard to go by train.
3 Paul: I'm going to visit China next year.
4 Porter: I'm sorry but the train left five minutes ago.
5 Robin suggested that Sarah should buy them the picture as a wedding present.
6 Sharon asked her mother if she knew where her tennis racquet was.
7 The boss warned him if he was late the next day he was going to sack him.
8 'It's my birthday the day after tomorrow.'
9 He said he had never flown before.
10 I was advised/told to take more exercise by my doctor.

p.108 LISTENING

1 Tapescript

Part A

PRESENTER: Our next caller is Rachel who is from South London. Go ahead, Rachel.
RACHEL: Hello, Doctor Howard.
DR HOWARD: Hello, Rachel. How can I help you?
RACHEL: Well, you see it's about my son, Mark. He's almost 18 and he hasn't been able to find a job since he left school.
DR HOWARD: When did he leave?
RACHEL: It'll be a year in July.
DR HOWARD: And what seems to be the problem?
RACHEL: It's like this. Mark used to be such a nice, outgoing sort of boy but over the last few months he's changed quite a bit.
DR HOWARD: So, can you describe what has happened?
RACHEL: Well, after he was turned down for several jobs he got depressed and withdrawn which was bad enough, but now it's got much worse – he's become really moody and aggressive.
DR HOWARD: Moody and aggressive?
RACHEL: Yes, and he's started mixing with some boys I don't like very much. But to tell you the truth, I think he's started taking drugs.
DR HOWARD: What makes you think that?
RACHEL: Well, as I said, there are his change of moods. One minute he's very depressed and the next minute he becomes very excited – you know, he can't sit still. Another thing is stuff has disappeared from the house. Some of my jewellry has gone and some money and so has Mark's cassette player.
DR HOWARD: Does he know you know about the cassette player?
RACHEL: Yes, he does. He told me he had let a friend borrow it. I was really surprised because he's always been so keen on music. When I asked him about it a couple of days later, he just told me to mind my own business. Another thing is that he just doesn't look after himself any more or care what he looks like. And I've noticed strange smells in the house too.
DR HOWARD: May I ask you, Rachel, are you still married?

RACHEL: Yes, I am but my husband spends a lot of time away. He's in the merchant navy, you see.

DR HOWARD: From what you've said, the change in your son has been quite dramatic. What I'd suggest is that you ...

Answers

1 True – *he hasn't been able to find a job since he left school.*
2 False – *a year in July*
3 True – *over the last few months he's changed quite a bit.*
4 False – *depressed and withdrawn ... moody and aggressive ...*
5 True – *... he's started mixing with some boys I don't like very much.*
6 False – *I think he's started taking drugs.*
7 False – *a cassette player*
8 True – *he's always been so keen on music.*
9 False – *some of my jewellry has gone and some money.*
10 True – *my husband spends a lot of time away.*

2 Tapescript

Part B

RACHEL: Yes, I am but my husband spends a lot of time away. He's in the merchant navy, you see.

DR HOWARD: From what you've said, the change in Mark has been quite dramatic and what I'd suggest is that you try and sit down with him and have a quiet chat about things. Approach him as a friend rather than as a mother. Try to get to the bottom of things and see how he feels. Something else which I would suggest is that you get in contact with one of his old teachers or your family doctor and ask them to have a chat with Mark. Someone he respects and could have a chat with.

RACHEL: And what if that doesn't work?

DR HOWARD: Well, if you do feel he is taking drugs, then I should contact the police.

RACHEL: Turn my own son in to the police!

DR HOWARD: It may seem harsh but it's probably the best course of action in the long run.

PRESENTER: OK, thank you Rachel. I hope things sort themselves out for you and Mark. Our next caller is ...

Answers

Dr Howard advises Rachel to:
1 try and talk things over with him as a friend.
2 ask one of his old teachers or family doctor to talk to him. Failing that, she recommends that Rachel tell the police.

pp.108–110 WRITING

1 You may first want to ask students to spend a few minutes drawing up a possible plan for this question in small groups. Then they should look at the sample answer and say what they think is good about it before getting down to analysing the mistakes in detail.

2 See page 56 for the corrected version.

3 Try and elicit the two points from the students before turning to the book.

pp.110–111 USE OF ENGLISH

1 Answers

1 loser;   2 loss;   3 lost;   4 lose;   5 lost

2 Answers

1 satisfying;   2 unsatisfactory;   3 dissatisfaction;
4 satisfied;   5 satisfying

3 Students should discuss their ideas together first before writing their answers.

This is a reasonably open question which allows the students flexibility in their answers. There are, however, constraints exerted by the competition rules. From the competition rules neither Jacinta Ryan nor Dilip Singh would be eligible for first or second prize because they are too young. Even though Julius Craig visits hospitals, he is not actually running a scheme of benefit to the community. He is an obvious choice, though, for second prize.

Here is a possible answer:

I think Cora McBride should win first prize because her work will help to find a solution to the problems of Northern Ireland. The only hope for the country is that young people learn to respect each other so they will live in peace when they grow up. She will need the money to help pay for holidays and community projects which will involve children from both groups.

Julius Craig deserves second prize for his outstanding bravery. He has shown people that it is possible to live with this terrible disease and is an example of hope to everyone. The prize will bring publicity to his case and encourage others to do more to help cancer sufferers.

My choice for third prize is Dilip Singh. Even though Andrea Cooper was brave too, Dilip Singh should receive the prize to show that society does not approve of racism and racist attacks. It is also important that someone from the youngest age group is among the prizewinners.

© Copyright Longman Group UK Ltd. 1989

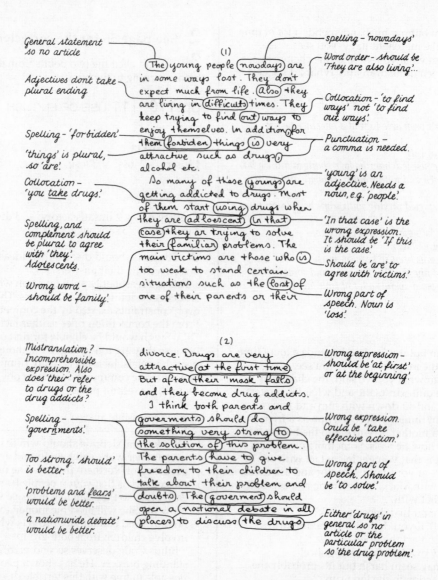

Revision quiz on Units 7–9

This can be done as a class quiz with students divided into teams. Questions should be asked of each team in turn. Two minutes should be allowed before one team spokesperson is required to answer the question. You should award between one and five points depending on how well the question has been answered. If the question has not been answered at all satisfactorily, it can be passed on to another group for a maximum of two bonus points.

1 What dangers does the earth face from sulphur dioxide/carbon monoxide/carbon dioxide?
2 Give the nouns for the following adjectives: *wide/ strong/high/weak/deep*.
3 Explain what is wrong in this sentence and why:
   A young man who lives the next door to me plays piano extremely well.
4 Make three appropriate sentences, each one including a different phrasal verb made from *turn*.
5 Describe a process, e.g. how something is made (using the passive appropriately).
6 Describe the personality and appearance of a well-known personality (to be assigned by yourself depending on the local context).
7 What are the opposites of: *sensitive/loyal/reliable/ patient/ responsible*.
8 Name five different reasons why you might decide **not** to buy a particular item of clothing you have been looking at in a clothes shop.
9 Describe five theories to explain teenage cults.
10 Put the following sentence into reported speech: *Why don't we go to the cinema straight after work tomorrow night like we did last Friday.*

UNIT 10

Us and Animals

Possible lesson organization

L1	SPEAKING	Quiz, p.112
	READING	Jungle warfare, pp.113–114
	LANGUAGE STUDY	The comparison of adjectives and adverbs, pp.114–115
	Homework	
	LANGUAGE STUDY	Sentences with **too** and **enough**, p.116

L2	LANGUAGE STUDY	Contrasting ideas, p.115
	SPEAKING	Describing a photograph, p.116
	WRITING	Opinion composition exs. 1–2, pp.116–117
	VOCABULARY	p.118
	Homework	
	WRITING	ex 3, p.117

L3	SPEAKING	Questionnaire, p.119
	LISTENING	Vivisection debate, p.119
	PRONUNCIATION	Sounds in sentences, p.120
	WRITING	Timed composition, p.120
	SPEAKING	Paper 5 exs. 1–3, pp. 120–121
	Homework	
	USE OF ENGLISH	exs. 1–2, p.122

p.112 SPEAKING

As a general introduction to the unit, you may wish to ask students what animals they especially like/dislike and why?

1 Animal quiz

Answers
1 whale;   2 cheetah;   3 field mouse;
4 black mamba;   5 ostrich;   6 Javanese rhinoceros;
7 mosquito (because it carries malaria – some experts, however, say it is the rat because of the bubonic plague its fleas carry.)

2 Our attitudes towards animals

Before ordering the animals according to beauty, you may wish to ask students to order them according to size as a further comprehension check. Having ordered the animals according to beauty, put students in pairs to explain their feelings and, if possible, to try and analyse why it is exactly that they find some animals more beautiful than others.

pp.113–114 READING
Jungle warfare

1 Before reading, to introduce the topic of the article, put students in small groups to come up with a list of the similarities and differences between humans and chimps. Groups then compare ideas in open class. You may also want to pre-teach the following items of vocabulary: *the wild, poke, cuddle, step-father.*

Answer
Both chimps and humans live in families, use tools, fight wars, are self-aware, have a kind of language, and under certain circumstances adopt.

2 **Answers**
1A *In this way she hopes to observe the progress of an entire generation of chimps from birth to death.*
2C *Nevertheless, older chimps may adopt younger brothers or sisters if the mother dies,* i.e. this is an *exceptional circumstance.*
3B *... there was no reason for the conflict other than a perhaps natural hostility to aliens*
4C see 2 C above
5C *Such research may give us clues about human behaviour and motivation.*

Extension
You could ask these questions: Did anything particularly surprise you in the article? What other animals have human characteristics?

pp.114–115 LANGUAGE STUDY
The comparison of adjectives and adverbs

1 **Answers**
1 correct
2 wrong – *James is **bigger** than Mark.*
3 wrong – *She is the **best** at English in our class.*
4 correct
5 wrong – *He plays tennis **well**.*
6 wrong – *His car isn't **as** good **as** mine.*
7 wrong – *She **hardly** works.* *Hardly means just a little.* Compare
He's breathing hard. (because he has just run up the stairs) and
He's hardly breathing. (Call a doctor!)
8 wrong – *You look **cold**.*
9 wrong – *They play chess much **worse** than us.*

2 Divide the class into groups with each group working on two or three of the questions. Distribute grammar reference books at the same time. When you have been round to check that all the groups have sorted out their questions and understood the principles involved, redivide the groups so that the students can, in each new group, between them explain the answers to all the questions to each other.

Answers
1 comparative – tall+er
  superlative – tall+est
2 comparative – more/less beautiful than
  superlative – the most/least beautiful
3 as + adj. + as
4

BASE	COMPARATIVE	SUPERLATIVE
good	better	the best
bad	worse	the worst
far	further/farther	the furthest/ the farthest

5 A slowly; B beautifully; C angrily;
  D hard/fast; E well
6 Comparative adverbs for *good* and *bad* are *better* and *worse*.
7 Normally adjectives have to go before nouns and adverbs after verbs. However, with verbs of perception like *look, feel, seem, sound, appear, smell* and *appear* we usually follow them with the adjective. But when we want to describe the way a verb is performed, i.e. its manner, we use an adverb. Compare *You look cold* and *He looked coldly at me.*
8 friendlier, cleverer

3 Use this exercise as a check that students have really understood the rules, so ask students to try it alone and then, afterwards, confer.

Answers
1 the youngest; 2 better; 3 as expensive;
4 the cheapest; 5 hard; 6 more slowly;
7 farther/further; 8 the worst; 9 the most/boring;
10 happy; 11 more beautifully; 12 less angry;
13 good; 14 more comfortable;
15 more quickly,faster

4 Put students in groups where the places they want to compare are the same.

p.115 LANGUAGE STUDY
Contrasting ideas

1 Before asking students to read the explanation in part 1 you may decide to put on the blackboard:
She had a cold. She still played tennis.
and this list: *although, but, even though, despite, however, nevertheless.*
Then ask them to connect the sentences with these link words.

1 correct
2 wrong – *Despite the fact that the restaurant ... Although the restaurant was ...*
3 wrong – *The wine was bad. However, the food was delicious.*
4 wrong – *We can't use **although** here because there is no contrast of ideas.*
5 wrong – *Even though he was rich, he was unhappy.*

3 Students should attempt this individually at first and then after a few minutes exchange their sentences with a partner to see if there are any mistakes before finally checking with you.

Possible answers
1 Despite its age /Even though it is very old, the dog really enjoys going for walks.
2 They have got a large dog although they have a small flat.
3 They tried to housetrain the puppy but it didn't work.
4 Pigs are supposed to be dirty. Nevertheless, they're quite clean.
5 The squirrels look tame. However, they may bite you.

p.116 LANGUAGE STUDY
Sentences with *too* and *enough*

Answers
1 Annie was too tired to take the dog for a walk.
2 The birdcage was too high up on the wall for the cat to reach.
3 The zebra was too slow/wasn't fast enough to escape the lion.
4 The dog is too stupid /isn't clever enough to learn that trick.
5 The children are too young/aren't old enough to have rabbits as pets.

p.116 SPEAKING
Describing a photograph

You may want to indicate the categories under which the examiners will be marking this part of the exam, i.e. fluency, grammatical accuracy, ability to communicate, range of vocabulary, and pronunciation at word and sentence level. Put students in pairs to describe the photograph. They take it in turns, one responding to the questions in the book and the other listening with the task of telling the first student their good points / areas for possible improvement in terms of the above categories. Then they swap roles and the second student now describes the photograph while the first student listens before commenting.

Commentary

The people in the picture are demonstrating against the use of fur to make coats. They are very serious-looking. The two women holding the placards could be sisters. The placard on the right reads *It takes up to 40 dumb animals to make a fur coat and only one to wear it.* The other placard reads *How would you like your fur, madam? Gassed, strangled, trapped or eletrocuted?*

pp.116–117 WRITING

1 Let students brainstorm the various questions in pairs and then put all the arguments, for and against, up on the blackboard. Pre-teach: *to breed / a trap*. Then ask students to read the composition quickly to find how many of the arguments they predicted are in the text and how many are not.

2 Understanding the organization of the composition

Answers
1 Topic vocabulary: fur, hunters, fashion, to breed, wild, savage, cruelty, traps, artificial.
2 A: first of all, then, to begin with, next; B: in addition, moreover; C: on the other hand; D: on balance, I believe
3 Both are adjectives. *Acceptable/Justifiable* mean possible to *accept/justify*. *Accepted/Justified* mean something has **already** been *accepted/justified*.

3 You may want to organize this as a mini-debate by dividing the class into groups of six (two in favour, two against, two or more audience). The debaters have five minutes to prepare their arguments. The audience should prepare questions they will ask at the end. The debaters speak alternately, i.e. one *for*, one *against*, one *for*, one *against*. There should be no questions or interruptions during the speeches. At the end the audience can ask questions. Finally, the audience votes for the sides that they agree with. Having done this, to tie everything together in preparation for the composition, elicit all the different arguments that were used during the debate and put them on the blackboard. There should also be a list of key vocabulary that students may need in writing the composition. Let students work on the plan together, putting students together who have largely similar viewpoints. You should go round helping and monitoring work on the plans.

p.118 VOCABULARY

1 Phrasal verbs in this unit

Answers
1 put down;   2 came across;   3 come up with;
4 broke out;   5 carry on;   6 back me up;
7 count on;   8 put forward;   9 turned on;
10 come about

2 Expressions with take + noun + preposition

Answers
1 part in;   2 care of;   3 pity on;   4 pride in;
5 advantage of

3 Expressions with preposition + noun + preposition

Answers
1 on account of; 2 in place of; 3 on behalf of;
4 by means of; 5 in addition to; 6 in answer to

Extension
Students take it in turns to contribute one sentence each to a story involving animals in some way. Each contribution must include one of the phrasal verbs or expressions just studied, so that the meaning makes sense in the context of the story and the sentence is grammatically correct.

p.119 SPEAKING

Divide the class into six groups, with one question each, to find the responses of the whole class to their one question. They might also want to note down additional comments – the most common – which they could report back in open class at the end.

p.119 LISTENING

Ask students to try and predict the answers to the questions **before** listening. Then listen to check their answers.

Tapescript
PRESENTER: Good morning everybody. I'm Joe Templer. It's eleven o'clock which means it's time for another edition of Crosstalk, the phone-in programme which looks at today's hot issues. The subject of today's discussion is whether vivisection – that's experimenting on live animals – is ever justified. Now if you want to take part in today's debate, the number to ring is 01 – if you're outside London – 833 3974. But before that, in the studio I have two guests to open the debate. They are Professor Anna Wright from Queen Margaret Hospital and Peter Savage of the Free the Animals Movement. Good morning to the both of you.
ANNA WRIGHT: Good morning.
PETER SAVAGE: Good morning.
PRESENTER: OK then, if you'd like to put your point of view first, Professor Wright.
ANNA WRIGHT: Thank you. Now I must state categorically that for advances in medicine we count on being able to carry out experiments on animals. Without them, there would be no progress. We are unable to observe human beings in scientifically

controlled conditions so unfortunately we have to rely on animals. Medicine has made enormous advances based on the results of vivisection. For example, our knowledge of the nervous system is largely due to vivisection. It has allowed us to find cures for many illnesses. Diptheria, smallpox and TB used to be killers in the old days but not any more. If you were bitten by a dog with rabies, you had very little chance of surviving. Now there is an antidote. Cancer recovery rates have greatly improved thanks to the work done on animals. And I'm afraid drugs have to be tested on animals prior to their release on the market to check for side effects. Nobody takes any pride in causing suffering and I can assure the listeners it is kept to an absolute minimum.

PRESENTER: Thank you very much, Professor Wright. Over to you, Peter.

PETER SAVAGE: ·Thanks. I'd like to start by saying that I'm speaking on behalf of animals. On the issue of testing drugs on animals for side effects in human beings, as we know from the thalidomide case, it's very difficult to predict what the effect of a drug will be on human beings from tests done on animals. They just don't tell us the whole story. As for understanding the nervous system, I think most experts would agree that this could have been done equally well by careful observation and nothing more. Professor Wright points to the reduction in the number of deaths from diseases like diptheria, TB and smallpox. This is utter nonsense because these diseases were in decline already and they've been on the decline primarily because of improvements in hygiene, not animal experiments. No, the whole thing is rubbish. If we look at penicillin and aspirin, two of the most famous modern drugs, these drugs were found by accident! So much for medical research! And Professor Wright's argument completely ignores the moral dimension. The point is experiments on animals should be stopped because they are cruel and inhumane. Dogs are made to smoke cigarettes and rats and mice have shampoo and cosmetics squirted in their eyes to see what will happen. Dogs don't smoke and mice don't wash their hair. Very often these animals have suffered so much they have to be put down. Basically, we should take care of animals not take advantage of them.

PRESENTER: Thanks, Peter. OK then. So it's over to you, the listeners. Our first call ...

Answers
1 We are unable to observe human beings in scientifically controlled conditions so unfortunately we have to rely on animals.
2 Diptheria, smallpox, TB and rabies.
  (Cancer recovery rates have improved but it would be an exaggeration to say that it had been conquered.)
3 To check for side effects.
4 It's very difficult to predict what the effect of a drug will be on human beings from tests done on animals.

5 These diseases were in decline already because of improvements in hygiene, not animal experiments.
6 These drugs were found by accident.
7 Experiments on animals are cruel and inhumane.

p.120 PRONUNCIATION
Sounds in sentences

1 Tapescript and Answers

1 It's eleven o'clock. *cateration*
   /r/ pronounced before the vowel
2 It's time for another edition of Crosstalk. /ə/
3 I have two guests to open the debate. *intrusive* /w/
4 I must state categorically. → *elision of /t/ in 'must'*
5 in the old days *elision of 'd' in 'old'* /ɪ/ *intrusive /j/ sound*
6 rats and mice /ə/ *elision of 'd'*

2 Answer

'Mr 'West 'used to be 'crazy about 'photography. 'One 'day /tə/ he 'took the 'car and 'went to a safari park. He 'stopped /w/ to 'take some 'pictures. 'Two ugly 'monkeys 'jumped on /ə/ /ə/ /w/ the 'car 'roof and 'bent the aerial. He got 'out of the 'car 'n' /j/ əv and 'tried to 'make them 'go away. 'Three enormous 'lions /w/ /j/ 'came and ate Mr 'West for 'lunch. /fə/

'	= stress
⌢	= linking
ʌ	= intrusive sound /w/ or /j/
X	= elision
/ə/	= schwa, weak form

p.120 WRITING

As exam practice, you may wish to do this as a timed (45 mins.) composition in class.

pp.120–121 SPEAKING

At this point in the course it is important to tell students where possible whether they will be having the interview in groups or individually.

1 Describing a photo

Put students into small groups of 'candidates' and 'examiners'. Candidates prepare what they are going to say; examiners prepare their questions. Monitor and assist both groups as necessary. The candidates should be reminded that above all it is their responsibility to keep the conversation going, to try and develop their answers, relating them to personal experience wherever possible. The examiners should be encouraged to prepare a range of questions, moving from more specific questions focussing on description of the picture to more general questions relating to the general subject of the picture. Examiners should also be reminded of the categories of assessment so that they have a basis for feedback at the end.

2 Commenting on a short text

Students should change roles for this exercise, so that candidates become examiners and vice versa. To keep in line with the actual exam, examiners should select one of the texts for the candidates to comment on. Give candidates and examiners about a minute to look at the text. You may want to tell candidates that if they cannot understand what they think is a key word/phrase in the text they should ask the examiner, e.g. *put down* in text D. This cannot affect their score adversely if done in appropriate and fluent English and will avoid candidates either panicking or making inappropriate comments on the text. To assist candidates in doing this effectively you may want to revise one or two expressions, e.g. *I'm sorry but I'm not sure of the exact meaning of* **to put down.**

Answers
A   from a manual on cat care
B   mother telling a small child off for not looking after the rabbit she so much wanted
C   car sticker protesting against the ill treatment of dogs
D   someone complaining about dogs – obviously a dog hater

3 Structured communication activity

Even if students will not be doing a group activity in Paper 5, this is good practice for Paper 3 Section B. If students will be doing Paper 5 in groups, you should monitor carefully, particularly to make sure that individual students are not dominating and that all are participating effectively. Give students a short amount of time to digest the information provided and perhaps sort out any problems with vocabulary before they begin.

Model answers
A dog would probably be suitable for Mr Cohen. He is active, enjoys long walks and has a house and garden in the country.
Mr Dukes probably needs a cat. Stroking cats can help to reduce your blood pressure, so they say!
Emma and Gemma can't have a kitten because of their mother's allergy. They aren't old enough for a dog and their garden is too small. A rabbit is possible but expensive. A hamster is the only suitable choice.
Elsie Grey should have a canary. Her flat is bright and sunny. The bird would sing and this would cheer the old lady up.

p.122 USE OF ENGLISH

You may decide to set these two exercises as homework but if not, one procedure for exploiting exercise 1 would be to firstly ask students to read through the text for the general idea, then attempt to complete it, either individually or in pairs. When this is done and the correct answers established, you may wish to ask students to deduce difficult vocabulary from the context. Students should then be asked to read it through one final time as preparation prior to telling the story to another student. When telling the stories, they should try and make it as interesting to the listener as possible with appropriate use of intonation, pauses and so on. When the students telling the story have finished, they should change pairs and those students who were the 'listeners' now tell the same story. For follow-up, find out if any students have any funny or strange animal stories to tell and put students in groups to listen to these, with one 'story-teller' per group. As back-up, in case no one is forthcoming with their own stories, you may want to have one of your own up your sleeve!

Answers
1 ago;   2 was;   3 off;   4 with;   5 up;   6 while;
7 hoped;   8 back;   9 however;   10 out;   11 on;
12 according;   13 saw;   14 of;   5 still;   16 in;
17 top;   18 on;   19 sure;   20 second

2

This could effectively be used in a following lesson as a revision test of the unit. Where problems arise, students should be referred back to the appropriate section of the unit.

Answers
1   Despite the fact that the dog barked all night, we still managed to sleep.
2   The mice run too fast for the cat to catch.
3   Dogs are more expensive to keep than cats.
4   There isn't an animal as cruel as man.
5   My canary doesn't sing as well as his.
6   Have you got any cheaper pet food?
7   Even though the winter was hard, most of the animals survived.
8   This is the dirtiest-looking dog I have ever seen!
9   The Persian cat was too expensive for her.
10 No animal runs as fast as the cheetah.

UNIT 11

Your Cultural Heritage

Possible lesson organization

L1	SPEAKING	Cleopatra's Needle, p.123
	READING	Carnival, pp.124–125
	LANGUAGE STUDY	**used to** and **would**, pp.125–126
	Homework	
	LANGUAGE STUDY	Prepositions following adjectives, p.126

L2	USE OF ENGLISH	Expanding a text, p.127
	WRITING	Making a speech exs 1–2, p.128
	VOCABULARY	**remind, remember** and **forget**, p.128
	*LANGUAGE STUDY	Adjective order, p.129
	LISTENING	In a museum, p.130
	Homework	
	WRITING	Making a speech ex. 3, p.128
	LANGUAGE STUDY	Verb patterns, p.128
	USE OF ENGLISH	ex. 1, p.128

L3	USE OF ENGLISH	King's College Chapel cloze, p.129
	SPEAKING	Describing a painting, pp. 131 and 132
	LISTENING	Describing a painting, p.131
	WRITING	Describing a painting, ex.1 p.132
	Homework	
	WRITING	ex.2 p.132

* This is the item that is most easily done by students at home if classroom time is short.

p.123 SPEAKING

1 Ask the class if they know what Cleopatra's Needle is and if they know anything about it. Students should then read the text quickly to check any ideas they had and to answer the questions in the book.

Answers
1 The obelisk came from Aswan in Egypt.
2 It was transported in a kind of cylindrical boat (a floating pontoon). During the journey seven sailors drowned.
3 various articles for future generations to study.

Extension
As further practice of sounds and word stress, you may like to put students in small groups to prepare to read the text aloud as if for a radio programme. They should each read part of the text. They should spend their preparation time deciding the appropriate pronunciation of individual words.

Having prepared and had assistance as necessary, each group should try reading out the text, with the other groups noting down any mistakes in pronunciation of sounds or word stress. Clearly, if this can be recorded, it will be possible to go back and listen again to any problematic areas. Don't worry too much about the intonation as this is something even native speakers would have problems with!

2 Discussion points
Questions 1 and 2 could be discussed in open class. But question 3 would be better done in small groups with each group suggesting five things they would choose and why. Having listened to all the arguments, the class could then vote on the best five from all those suggested.

p.124 READING

1/2 As an introduction, you may wish to ask the class what Carnival is, where it comes from, what the origins of the word are and who took Carnival to the New World. Students should then quickly scan *Carnival Facts* for the answers. Before reading Joe Grayson's description of the Trinidadian carnival, perhaps pre-teach *cane* and *bamboo stem*. Students should read through Joe's description quickly to summarize with a partner at the end, then look at the multiple choice questions and finally go back to the text to find the parts which answer the questions.

Answers
1C see CARNIVAL FACTS
2D *... the black population of Trinidad used to be slaves.*
3A *... which started at midnight on the Sunday.*
4C *... the beating of real drums was banned.*
5B *... none of them can match the scale of the Trinidadian festival.*

3 With multi-lingual groups, put students from the same place together to prepare a talk. When this is done, each group presents and then answers questions from the other students. With monolingual groups, students should be put in small groups, each one preparing to talk about a different festival. After the presentations, **you** should be prepared to ask follow-up questions.

pp.125–126 LANGUAGE STUDY
used to and *would*

1 To get the students thinking about the distinctions between the above two target structures, put the following sentences on the blackboard for students to decide which are grammatically possible and which are not:

When I was younger	*I used to go to the cinema every Friday night.*
	I would to go to the cinema every Friday night.
	I would go to the cinema every Friday night.
	I used to be quite fat.
	I would to be quite fat.
	I would be quite fat.

When they have done this and had the answers checked, they should think about the rules before reading the explanation in part 1. We cannot say *His father **would work** at the car factory* because it refers to a state.

2 To do this as a 'Spot the difference' information-gap game, divide the class into A/B pairs. A covers the top picture and B covers the bottom picture. Through discussion and by asking questions about each other's pictures, they attempt to find as many differences as possible. They should then (before referring to the other's picture) tell you how things have changed. Finally, they can refer to the other picture to see what they missed, if anything.

Extension
To personalize this section, ask students to describe to each other ways in which their lives have significantly changed over the years. You may like to start off by telling them how life has changed for you, as an example.

p.126 LANGUAGE STUDY
Prepositions following adjectives

Answers
1 in;   2 at;   3 of;   4 for;   5 at;   6 by;   7 about;
8 to;   9 of;   10 for;   11 with;   12 from/to;
13 on;   14 for;   15 for/about

p.127 USE OF ENGLISH
Expanding a text

1

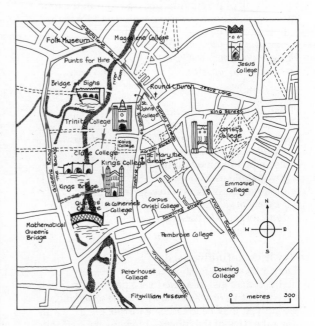

2 Answer

Good morning, ladies and gentlemen. Please allow me to introduce myself. My name is Amanda Southgate and I would like to welcome you to the wonderful town of Cambridge on behalf of Culture Tours. I am/will be your guide today and it gives/will give me great pleasure to introduce you to the most important sights in this town.

We are going to start the/our tour here at the Round Church, one of the few round churches in England. After that, we visit/shall/are going to visit Trinity and Clare Colleges and then walk along the back of the colleges to admire the daffodils which are now in bloom. Then we visit/shall/are going to/visit King's College and its beautiful chapel. After a brief look at Queen's College, we stop/shall/are going to stop for a picnic lunch. Please may I remind you not to walk on the grass and keep to the footpath.

This afternoon there is a visit to the Folk Museum which shows how people used to live in the old days. Finally, there will be an opportunity for you to experience a trip on a punt, which is a kind of boat you push along with a pole. I wouldn't recommend you trying it yourself as it's easy to fall in the river!

One last thing I would like to say before we begin the tour is if anyone should get lost, don't forget to be back here at the Round Church by 4.30 in order to catch the coach back. Many thanks for being so patient. Now let us begin the tour.

63

p.128 WRITING
Making a speech

1 Useful expressions

Virtually all of paragraphs one and four in the tour guide speech. From paragraphs two and three the following may be used at other times:
We are going to start our tour here ...
This afternoon there is a visit to ...
There will be an opportunity for you to experience ...

2

Please allow me *to introduce* myself.
I would like *to welcome* you ...
It gives me great pleasure *to introduce* you to ...
... *to admire* the daffodils
Please may I remind you not *to walk* ...
... how people used *to live*...
... an opportunity for you *to experience* ...
... it's easy *to fall* ...
... don't forget *to be* back here ...
... in order *to catch* ...

Why is the infinitive used?
There are various reasons:
Firstly, it may just be a fixed verb pattern, e.g. *would like* + infinitive or *remind someone to do something*.
Secondly, it may be to indicate **purpose**, e.g. ... walk along the back of the colleges *to admire* the daffodils.
Thirdly, it may suggest futurity,
e.g. ... *don't forget to be back here* ...
cf. *I'll never forget meeting you* where the gerund is used to make a reference backwards in time.

3
This would best be set as homework, though you may like to allow some preparation time in class. (Again, in multilingual classes students from the same cities should prepare together.) The following lesson students should roleplay being the tour guide and tourists who ask appropriate questions.

p.128 VOCABULARY
remind, remember and *forget*

1 Answers

1 forget;   2 remind;   3 remember;   4 remember;
5 remind;   6 reminded

Extension
You may also want to bring up the difference in meaning between *He remembered to lock the door* and *He remembered locking the door*. Other verbs which alter their meaning in this way depending on whether used in the gerund or the infinitive are *forget/stop/go on/ regret*. (As Swan remarks in *Practical English Usage* the *-ing* form refers to things that happened earlier, i.e. **before** the remembering or forgetting take place while the infinitive refers to things that happen **after** the remembering.)

2
This could easily and effectively be done as a role play. Explain the situation to the class and then distribute the role cards. Give students time to absorb the information and let them ask about anything they do not understand.

ROLE CARD ONE
You are a rather anxious individual, always checking that other people have understood exactly what you mean. You know that your friend is a little careless and has a tendency to forget important details but he/she is the only person you know who can help out at the moment. You must explain very carefully about how he/she must look after some exotic foreign plants which react badly to the wrong amounts of water and light. You also have some temperamental goldfish and an antique table is being delivered. You want to be sure that the table has not been damaged during transportation.

ROLE CARD TWO
Your friend is very nice but worries far too much about anything and everything. He/She also tends to repeat everything three or four times quite unnecessarily which can get rather irritating. You, in fact, are very busy at the moment with work and it is not easy to find time to do all the things your friend wants you to do. You would be quite happy if someone else took care of the flat while he/she was away.

© Copyright Longman Group UK Ltd. 1989

p.128 LANGUAGE STUDY

Answers
1 Sophie invited Ann to come to the art gallery.
2 Leila persuaded me to go to the *son et lumière* show.
3 His mother encouraged him to visit the ruins that afternoon.
4 The guide warned me/us/them not to walk on the grass.
5 The curator ordered me/us to stop smoking at once.

pp.128–129 USE OF ENGLISH

1 Answers

1 Her landlady advised her to take a picnic.
2 It took thirty years for them to put in those windows.
3 She reminded John to tip the guide.
4 The child was warned not to touch the vase.
5 The castle used to be lived in.
6 Smoking is not allowed/permitted in here.
7 The tour lasted three hours.
8 The king had the chapel decorated by Italian craftsmen.

2 Answers

1 without; 2 most; 3 over/nearly/about/almost;
4 example; 5 built; 6 next/following; 7 the;
8 its; 9 can; 10 from; 11 them; 12 also;
13 by; 14 which; 15 shows; 16 for; 17 and;
18 at; 19 queue/wait; 20 is

p.129 LANGUAGE STUDY
Adjective order

1 In order to make sure students understand the vocabulary so that they are fully focussed on the grammar in the following exercises, you may wish to put the following categories on the blackboard and brainstorm vocabulary which comes under each heading: *size, pattern, material, shape.*
All the vocabulary that comes up in exercises 1 and 2 should be included.

Answers
1 She is wearing a green French cotton running vest.
2 George plays with a black American graphite tennis racquet.
3 She was given a pair of blue Swiss plastic ski boots.

2 Answers

1 an antique oak English writing desk
2 one eighteenth century silver Bavarian beer mug
3 a delightful small gold and silver French Louis XV clock
4 a pair of ancient Italian duelling pistols
5 a dirty-looking tiger skin rug
6 a tiny green stone Columbian statue
7 an ugly old deep rectangular trunk
8 two pairs of blue and white striped silk pyjamas

p.130 LISTENING

As an introduction, ask students what kind of museums they like, what they think are the features of a good museum, what they think about charging an entrance fee for museums.

Tapescript
CURATOR: Hello everybody. I'm glad you've been able to make it. It's a shame about the weather though, isn't it? Anyway, if you'd like to follow me into the first room, I'll tell you a little bit about some of the exhibits there. Well, as you can see, there are a number of farming and domestic implements here which we have collected over the years. Of course, none of them are used any longer. In actual fact, we can sometimes have quite a job finding out just exactly what they were for! Now this first one I suppose you'd describe as a giant comb. And that's just what it is - not for human beings, though, but for wool. Once the wool had been sheared from the sheep, then it would have to be combed to make it ready for spinning. Now if you look over here, you

can see something which looks just like a huge frying pan with a very long handle. We had an Italian visitor in here last year who thought it was for baking pizza in a deep oven but it's actually a warming pan. In the old days you'd pop it into your bed to make it nice and warm. You'd take some coals from the fire or a hot brick, then you'd put it into the copper pan and make sure the lid was tight. Then, as I say, pop it in the bed. This one is an original but I should warn you about some of the ones you may come across in antique shops. They're quite often reproductions. So don't be taken in.

Now, this next object is rather strange-looking. It is called a flail and, as you can see, it is a couple of poles of about equal length which are held together by a strap. Now this was used before the days of modern agricultural machinery to beat the corn to separate the wheat from the chaff, the bits you didn't want. The men used to put the cut corn on the ground and then they'd swing the flail and beat it until they had separated all the wheat out.

The last thing in this room I want to draw your attention to before we move on to our Roman collection is this evil-looking contraption in the corner. Now this is in fact a *man* trap. It just shows how much crueller the world was in the nineteenth century. Farm workers and their families often had very little to eat and so to supplement their meagre diets they would go onto the farm owner's land to hunt for rabbits and other game, poaching in other words. And the farm owners would set these traps to stop them from doing this. Not very pleasant. And if someone did get caught in a trap, then their leg would certainly have been broken. After that, it would be a short step from the courthouse onto one of those terrible prison ships bound for Australia.

Answers
1

	NAME	USE
object 1	comb	combing wool (for spinning)
object 2	warming pan	warming the bed
object 3	flail	separating the wheat from the chaff
object 4	trap	catching poachers

2B *It's a shame about the weather ...*
3D *... we can sometimes have quite a job finding out exactly what they were for.*
4D *... looks just like a huge frying pan with a very long handle*
5A *... it is a couple of poles of about equal length which are held together by a strap*
6C *After that, it would be a short step from the courthouse onto one of those terrible prison ships bound for Australia.*

p.131 SPEAKING
Describing a painting

1 Ask students to describe the painting themselves before reading the text.

2 Answers

1 The small girl is *saying something to the other one* ... *it was* painted maybe a hundred years ago.

2 *I can see* can be replaced *by there is/are*.
Maybe can be replaced by *I think, probably, it, might have* or *it looks as though*, depending on the context.

3 *in the foreground/background* ...
It might have been painted x years ago ...
It's similar in style to Van Gogh/Rembrandt.

4/5 See the *Listening* tapescript below.

p.131 LISTENING

WOMAN: This is a painting of a country scene. I think it was probably painted about a hundred years or so ago. Anyway, in the foreground there are two girls. They both look very poor. Their clothes are old and shabby, and there's tears and patches in them. They are sitting by the side of a field and, well I suppose they look as though they are having a rest. The elder of the two girls has got some sort of oh, I think it's an old-fashioned accordion. She's young, quite pretty with red hair. She's sitting with her eyes half closed, most likely because of the sun. In the background there are fields with a few animals in them and some farm buildings on the top of the hill and the most beautiful rainbow in the sky. It must have been raining but the sky is quite dark and it looks as though it might rain again. The little girl is quite enchanted by the rainbow. She seems to be telling her friend, or perhaps it's her sister, to have a look too. The other girl doesn't appear to be that interested. Oh, wait a minute. She's got something around her neck. It says 'Pity the blind.' I see. I get it. The elder of the two girls is blind and the younger one is trying to tell her about the rainbow. Quite sad really. The colours of the painting are marvellous. Just like you get after it's been raining. There's so much beauty all around but all the blind girl can feel is the warmth of the sun on her face. She can't even appreciate the butterfly which has settled on her. I suppose she must play the accordion and hope that people give her money. Yes, it's a lovely painting, it's lovely, although in general I'm not a fan of this kind of art. I prefer Impressionist pictures, people like Monet, Cezanne. I recently went to see a big exhibition ...

Answers

1 A – *I can see* is replaced by *there are*.
   – *Maybe* is replaced by *I think, probably, they look as though, she seems to be* and *I suppose*.
   B *in the foreground* and *in the background*

2 the weather, the clothes the girls wear, when it was painted, her reaction to the painting and her own general preferences in relation to art

3 See the last part of the tapescript.

p.132 SPEAKING

Encourage students to put into practice the structures and vocabulary that have been discussed with reference to the Millais painting.

p.132 WRITING

1 With this text you may like to put students in small groups to analyse the particularly good aspects, encouraging them to highlight any words or phrases that they think they may want to use in the homework.

2 This can be set as homework.

UNIT 12

Crime and Society

Possible lesson organization

L1	SPEAKING	Questionnaire, p.133
	READING	A life of crime, pp. 134–135
	LANGUAGE STUDY	Conditional sentences using **if**, pp.135–136
	PRONUNCIATION	Conditional sentences, p.136
	*LANGUAGE STUDY	Verbs followed by prepositions, pp.136–137
	Homework	
	VOCABULARY	Paper 1: Reading comprehension Section A, p.139

L2	*VOCABULARY	Phrasal verbs and Different types of crime, p.137
	SPEAKING	Paper 5 Structured communication activity, p.138
	WRITING	The opinion question, pp.142–143
	Homework	
	WRITING	ex. 2 p.143

L3	SPEAKING	Discussing texts, p.140
	LANGUAGE STUDY	Ways of saying **if**, p.140
	LANGUAGE STUDY	Forms of **wish**, pp.140–141
	*USE OF ENGLISH	Cloze, p.142
	LISTENING	p.141
	*USE OF ENGLISH	Sentence transformations, p.143
	Homework	
	USE OF ENGLISH	Written report on drinking and driving statistics, p.138

These are the items that are most easily done by students at home if classroom time is short.

p.133 SPEAKING
You and your scruples

You may wish to pre-teach *to beat, to scratch, a tramp*. Having done this, give the class time to complete the questionnaire, adding their own fourth options. While this is going on, monitor carefully, giving assistance as necessary. Students should then pair up and compare

responses and particularly any new alternatives they have created. Any really interesting ones could be read out to the whole class.

Alternatively, put students into groups of three or four, purely to work on creating interesting fourth alternatives. When they have done this, they should give their questionnaire to members of another group. So, in the next stage every student is completing the questionnaire of another group. Having completed it, students should compare results within their original group. They may also, afterwards, be interested to give and receive feedback regarding the student-created fourth alternatives.

pp.134–135 READING
A Life of Crime

1 Put a time limit of about two minutes on the first read-through and then, without referring back to the text, let students discuss their ideas on the questions.

Answers
1 her upbringing, the death of her mother, her cruel stepmother, hunger
2 clearly subjective – should generate class discussion

2 Now let the class read through the text again carefully. As usual, encourage them to mark the parts of the text which support/justify their choice of answer. To encourage open class discussion, stand at the blackboard and elicit *the class's* answer to each question. Each answer must be unanimously agreed before it is put on the blackboard. Any disagreement must not be ignored but discussed until resolved. If at the end the class has agreed on any wrong answers, show them where they went astray.

Answers
1D *a sharp-eyed store detective*
2D *Hunger drove young Rose to steal food.*
3C *Myra Hindley ... would have certainly followed Ellis to the scaffold if hanging had not been abolished.*
4A *opportunity to go straight*
5B *popularity of credit cards ... people tend to carry less cash around*

3 Discussion points
This can either be done in groups with open class feedback at the end or with more of a debate style format.

pp.135–136 LANGUAGE STUDY
Conditional sentences using *if*

1 Having conferred in groups and had the correct form of each conditional confirmed by you, students should attempt to analyse the differences in meaning resulting from the use of each conditional **before** looking at exercise 2.

Answers

1 If it rains, we will not play tennis.
2 If he had a haircut, he would look nicer.
3 If she had phoned you, I would have told you.

2 Students should also try and come up with other examples of their own to demonstrate they have grasped the significance of the way the different conditionals are used.

Answers

A 2; B 5; C 4; D 1; E 3

3 It is best if students attempt this on their own at first to help them see if they really have understood the grammar.

Answers

1 What would you do if you were in my situation?
2 If you do that again, you'll have to go to bed.
3 If he'd been less mean, she wouldn't have left him.
4 If we leave now, we'll miss the rush hour traffic.
5 If you smoked less, you'd have much more money.
6 If we'd locked the car window, we wouldn't have given them the opportunity to break in.
7 When Alice gets here, will you show her to her room?
8 ... what would you say if I gave you a little present?
9 If you press that button, a receptionist will come to help you.
10 If you'd come with us, you would have enjoyed it too.
11 Imagine, darling. What would we do if your husband had an accident?
12 If I were the Prime Minister, I'd bring back capital punishment.

p.136 PRONUNCIATION

1 Answers

1 I'll *do* it if you *want* me to.
2 If he hadn't *come*, we'd've had a good *time*.
3 If I were *you*, I'd see a *doctor*.
4 If *only* I hadn't *said* it.

Extension
Having considered what would generally be contracted in normal speech, you may like to discuss with students when you would **not** make these contractions, e.g. in formal writing, when you specifically want to stress the contracted word and so on. Equally, having elicited the appropriate sentence stress given a *neutral* speech situation, you may want to ask students to see how many different ways it would actually be feasible to stress these sentences and to analyse the consequent effect on meaning, recalling the earlier work on shifting stress done in Unit 2.

2 When the students have sorted out which conditional is being used in each case, you may want to get them to take down each sentence as dictation.

Tapescript

1 I'd have come if I'd known.
2 Would you mind if he borrowed Dave's car?
3 What'll we do if the police come?
4 If we hadn't done that, we'd be all right.
5 I'll tell him if you threaten me.
6 We'd have plenty of money if we'd been insured.
7 I wouldn't do that if I were you.
8 If only you'd told me, I wouldn't have said it.

Answers

	FIRST	SECOND	THIRD	MIXED
1			✓	
2		✓		
3	✓			
4				✓
5	✓			
6				✓
7		✓		
8			✓	

pp.136–137 LANGUAGE STUDY
Verbs followed by prepositions

1 Answers

1 of; 2 for; 3 for; 4 from; 5 for; 6 for;
7 from; 8 of; 9 on; 10 about

2 Answers

1 Her employer accused her of stealing money.
2 Rose blames her parents for not bringing her up properly.
3 His mother punished him for being rude to their neighbour.
4 The lock prevented the burglar from breaking into the house.
5 The jury convicted him of murdering his wife.
6 The shopkeeper forgave the child for stealing the sweets.
7 His son was/has been arrested for selling drugs to teenagers.
8 Her nephew was discouraged from talking to the police.
9 The judge congratulated the police on catching the gang.
10 She warned the children about playing in the park after dark.

p.137 VOCABULARY
Phrasal verbs

You could focus the class's attention on the phrasal verbs in the box at the bottom **before** they attempt the exercise, asking them in groups to explain the meaning of any of the phrasal verbs they recognize, and, where possible, giving an example sentence. Having done this, let them try the exercise, and afterwards encourage them to learn any of the phrasal verbs which they had not previously known (at least with the particular meanings in this text). Note that these are five unconnected paragraphs.

Answers
1 looking into; 2 held up; 3 got away with;
4 ran over; 5 made for; 6 made up;
7 take everyone in; 8 found out; 9 gave her away;
10 up to; 11 broke down; 12 let him off;
13 went off; 14 break into

Different types of crime

1/2

Either let students read the descriptions of the crimes and match up the names given in the box at the bottom **or** write the names of the crimes on the board in random order and then read the descriptions out loud, one by one. Students in groups confer and then suggest which crime you are referring to. Having done this, you may wish to draw up a table on the blackboard for students to complete:

CRIME	CRIMINAL	ACT
1 blackmail	a blackmailer	to blackmail
2 vandalism	a vandal	to vandalize

Answers

	CRIME	CRIMINAL	ACT
3	mugging	a mugger	to mug
4	shoplifting	a shoplifter	to shoplift
5	burglary	a burglar	to burgle
6	rape	a rapist	to rape
7	arson	an arsonist	to commit arson
8	forgery	a forger	to forge
9	fraud	–	to defraud
10	kidnapping	a kidnapper	to kidnap
11	drug pushing	a drug pusher	to push drugs
12	terrorism	a terrorist	to commit an act of terrorism
13	smuggling	a smuggler	to smuggle

Extension
Afterwards, students can test each other on the vocabulary by giving each other mini-situations as in exercise 1 from which they must identify the crime, the criminal or the act. Alternatively, they could rank the crimes, selecting the three most/least serious ones.

p.138 SPEAKING
Paper 5 Structured communication activity

Give the class time to read through the different cases and sort out any problematic vocabulary. Then divide the class into small groups to discuss who should go free. For groups that finish more quickly than others you might ask them to agree on appropriate sentences for the three who actually remain in prison. At the end each group should explain what they decided and why.

p.138 USE OF ENGLISH

This is probably best set as homework.

> **Model answer**
> Over the past 18 months the number of accidents has increased. The groups most at risk are the young and the older age group over 60. The main reasons for accidents seem to be road conditions for the old and alcohol for the young. I predict that this winter the number of serious accidents will be higher if we have the bad weather which is expected. In order to reduce accidents this winter we should send a poster to all companies which are going to have office parties to warn against the dangers of drinking and driving. Police officers should visit pubs and discos so that youngsters are aware that the police are watching. Old people should be encouraged to think twice before going out. I will organize an interview on local radio and TV to warn about the dangers that motorists face. Lastly, I will advise magistrates to be strict with drunken drivers.
>
> © Copyright Longman Group UK Ltd 1989

p.139 VOCABULARY
Paper 1 Section A

Answers
1A; 2D; 3A; 4D; 5D; 6B; 7D; 8C; 9B; 10B; 11 A;
12D; 13A ; 14D; 15B; 16B; 17B; 18D; 19C; 20A; 21C;
22A ; 23D; 24D; 25B

p.140 SPEAKING
Discussing texts

1 Answers

A Wayne encouraging his friend to have another drink
B magistrate reading the sentence of the court
C father talking to son
D Jerry reflecting on events

2 Answers

1 Order of texts: C, A, B, D
2 Between the texts the boys had an accident and Wayne was arrested for drinking and driving.
3 Jerry is a little shaken up but wants to pass on the blame to his friend, Wayne. Wayne is irresponsible. The father is probably too soft.

Extension

With classes that enjoy role play and freer speaking activities, you might like to put students in groups of four to work out a sketch based round the information in the texts. The sketch would probably have a number of quite short scenes. One student should play Wayne, one should play Jerry, one should play the father and one should be the director. Set a time limit for preparation, e.g. 20 minutes and then let students perform in front of each other. The performances could be recorded (either on video or cassette) and then gone through with particularly good sections highlighted and any areas of difficulty discussed and analysed.

p.140 LANGUAGE STUDY
Ways of saying *if*

Answers

1 A ... *as long as* you drive slowly.
  B ... *otherwise* you will go to jail.
  C ... *provided* you promise to be careful.
  C ... *unless* you want to lose your licence.
2 A unless; B as long as; C provided; D otherwise
3 In these particular contexts *unless* gives a **reason** for not doing something, i.e. having the picnic, whereas *otherwise* gives the **consequence** of not doing something, i.e. missing the train.

pp.140–141 LANGUAGE STUDY
Forms of *wish*

1 Answers

1 A present/future – an imaginary situation
  B He thinks it's unlikely.
2 A present/future
  B The wish is impossible.
3 A He didn't wear gloves.
  B If we imagine a burglar is speaking, he is probably pretty fed up. The police probably caught him because he left his fingerprints.
4 A Both.
  B No, she doesn't.
  C She finds it annoying.
  D Not really.
5 A Both; B Yes; C We don't know
6 A No; B Yes

2 Answers

1 I wish I had a bigger flat.
2 I wish I could lose weight.
3 I wish I had insured my fur coat.
4 I wish he wouldn't whistle.
5 I wish I hadn't drunk so much last night.
6 I wish I could open this bottle.
7 I wish Angus would ring.

Note

Make sure students remember that they can't use the *I wish + would* construction to talk about themselves.

p.141 LISTENING

1
Pre-teach: *a kid, a fellow, a lollipop lady, to chat, an ice-cream van.*

Tapescript

WOMAN A: Have you heard the news?
WOMAN B: No.
WOMAN A: There's been an accident up near the school.
WOMAN B: Oh dear.
WOMAN A: Yes, Mark Brown, Jackie Brown's kid – you know who I mean, don't you?
WOMAN B: Yes, bit of a dreamer, always in a world of his own.
WOMAN A: That's right. Anyway, Mark's been knocked over by a car.
WOMAN B: Oh, is he badly hurt?
WOMAN A: Well, it could have been a lot worse. He's been taken to hospital with suspected concussion but no broken bones as far as I know. I expect they'll keep him in for a few days just to keep an eye on him.
WOMAN B: Well, how did it happen then?
WOMAN A: It seems that some fellow in a Jaguar ran him over as he was crossing the road outside the school.
WOMAN B: It's a terrible corner that one near the school. There's always such a lot of traffic. But wasn't there someone there to supervize the children crossing the road?
WOMAN A: Apparently not. It seems the lollipop lady was off sick and, to make matters worse, Jason's class teacher had let them out ten minutes early because he wasn't feeling well. Can you believe it?
WOMAN B: Well, that's very irresponsible.
WOMAN A: That's what I said.
WOMAN B: But what about Mark's mum? Wasn't she meant to be picking him up?
WOMAN A: In fact, it was his dad who was picking him up and he was late 'cause he'd been chatting with some of his mates.
WOMAN B: Typical!
WOMAN A: Isn't it just. Anyway, it's Mark's fault as much as anybody's.
WOMAN B: Why's that?

WOMAN A: Apparently, he just rushed across the road without looking to get to the ice-cream van and around the corner comes this Jaguar and – bang! – Mark's in hospital.

WOMAN B: Was the driver going too fast?

WOMAN A: Yes, late for his appointment, I'm told.

WOMAN B: Do you think he'll have to go to court?

WOMAN A: Oh, I'm sure he will. He was being breathalized by a policeman when I arrived.

WOMAN B: Mind you. That sort always get off.

woman a: Well, I'm not so sure it was his fault. Anyway, the lucky thing was there was a nurse walking past when it all happened and she was able to give Mark first aid treatment until the ambulance arrived. So that was a bit of luck, wasn't it?

Answers
1 False – *a bit of a dreamer*
2 False – *suspected concussion* (only)
3 True – *I expect they'll keep him in for a few days.*
4 True – *It seems that some fellow in a Jaguar ran him over as he was crossing the road outside the school.*
5 Not stated – *He was being breathalized ...*
6 False – *a nurse ... was able to give Mark first aid*
7 False – *it was his dad who was picking him up.*
8 False – *he just rushed across the road ... to get to the ice-cream van*

3 **Example sentences**
DRIVER: *I wish I hadn't been driving so fast.*
MARK: *I wish I hadn't run across the road without looking.*
JASON'S TEACHER: *I wish I hadn't let the children out early.*
MARK'S DAD: *I wish I hadn't been late.*

p.142 USE OF ENGLISH

Answers
1 just; 2 handing/giving; 3 would; 4 that;
5 turned; 6 who; 7 demanding; 8 own;
9 raised/sounded; 10 hand; 11 Even; 12 easy;
13 leave/escape; 14 rather; 15 in; 16 The;
17 usually; 18 extremely; 19 despite; 20 a

pp.142–143 WRITING
The opinion question

1/2 Put students into small groups to brainstorm any ideas they have for points they might want to include in such a composition. They should then try and sort them into paragraphs and decide on an appropriate framework for their composition. Having done this, tell them to read the two example compositions and hold an open-class discussion where students express their views on the relative merits of the two compositions. When their best elements have been highlighted, give students a little time to discuss how they might alter/add to their original plan. From this plan, students should write the composition at home or, to give practice in writing under exam-like pressure, immediately in class with a time limit of approximately 35 minutes as they have already had planning time.

Comments on the two compositions
Both compositions have good ideas. However, the sentence structure and range of expression of the essay on p.142 is more sophisticated and varied. It uses ways of balancing and introducing arguments appropriate to this type of subject. In addition, the vocabulary of the first composition is much broader. Between the two essays there is a very good selection of ideas and topic vocabulary.

p.143 USE OF ENGLISH

Answers
1 Unless you change your ways, you are going to end up in prison.
2 If I were you, I'd call the police.
3 He suggested that we should fit new locks on the door.
4 If he had worn gloves, the police wouldn't have caught him.
5 She wishes she had insured the stereo.
6 Our house was broken into while we were on holiday.
7 I'll call the police if you like/if you want me to.
8 As I didn't know all the facts, I rang the police.
9 Jerry can't have stolen the jewels because he didn't know where the key to the safe was.
10 Provided you fill the car up with petrol, you can borrow it.

Revision exercise for Units 10–12

Divide the class into three groups and allocate each group one of the three previous units. Give them between 20–30 minutes to make up a test for the other two groups based on the material in their unit. You should be on hand to help, make suggestions and explain where necessary. When the three tests are ready, each group takes it in turn to play quizmaster while the other two groups attempt to answer the questions.

UNIT 13

Beyond belief

Possible lesson organization

L1	SPEAKING	p.144
	LISTENING	The Chaffin Will affair, p.144
	READING	Imaginary friends, pp.144–146
	*VOCABULARY	Ways of looking, p.146
	*LANGUAGE STUDY	Abbreviating clauses, pp.146–147

L2	LISTENING	Reincarnation, p.147
	PRONUNCIATION	p.147
	*LANGUAGE STUDY	**no sooner** and **not only**, pp 147–148
	VOCABULARY	Extreme adjectives, p.148
	WRITING	The narrative essay exs. 1–2, p.149
	Homework	
	WRITING	ex.3, p.149

L3	READING	Understanding the mysteries of intuition, pp.150–151
	USE OF ENGLISH	Cloze, p.151
	VOCABULARY	Multiple choice, p.152

These are the items that are most easily done by students at home if classroom time is short.

p.144 SPEAKING

Put students in groups to describe what they can see in the opening picture.
As usual, encourage students to develop their responses to the questions, not just *Yes/No* answers but giving reasons, arguments, personal experience where possible. To bring the discussion to a conclusion you may like to ask the class to come up with a list of reasons why certain people believe in ghosts, are superstitious and so on.

p.144 LISTENING
The Chaffin Will affair

1 Tapescript and Answer

One of the most famous and extraordinary cases of contact with the dead was the so-called Chaffin Will affair. In 1921 a certain James Chaffin died leaving his entire fortune to his third son, Marshall, in a will which had been written a full 15 years earlier in 1905

and signed in front of witnesses. His wife and two other sons were virtually cut off without a penny. Marshall was not inclined to split up the inheritance he had come into any more fairly. Four years went by and then, strangely, James Chaffin's ghost started to appear before one of his other two sons. The apparition had on an old overcoat which Chaffin had often worn in life. On the ghost of Chaffin's second visit to his son*, he told him that he would find a will in the overcoat pocket. The coat was actually in the possession of the third brother. Once it was found, they came across a note sewn in the lining of one of the pockets saying they should look in an old family bible. This bible was found in the keeping of Chaffin's widow and examined in front of independent witnesses. Sure enough, there in the bible they discovered a later version of the will, one which divided the property and money up evenly between the widow and the three sons. The will appeared to be genuine and Marshall was not prepared to challenge it in court.

*The speaker means 'on the second visit of Chaffin's ghost to his son'.

2 Answers

1 True – *He didn't want to share out the money more fairly.*
2 True – *It was written in 1905.*
3 True – *Four years after Chaffin's death in 1921.*
4 False – *No, only to her sons.*
5 True – *It said the will could be found in the overcoat.*
6 False – *It was in the bible.*
7 True – *She looked after it so we can assume it was hers.*
8 False – *No, a quarter. They shared it with their mother too.*

pp.144–146 READING
Imaginary friends

1 Pre-teach: *pushchair, lad, to tuck someone in, commotion, stretcher.* You may also want to introduce the idea of *imaginary friends* by asking the class if they ever had any as children or if they knew any children that did. Do they think it is bad for children to fantasize in this way?

Answers

1 Imaginary friends come from the spirit world.
2 They helped her with her maths exams.
3 Her earliest experience was when she was four.

2 Answers

1A *One dad wrote to me to say he was getting very worried ...*
2D *... there's nothing frightening about children having imaginary friends, especially if they've been very close.*
3D *... but Christopher and Pansy helped me to pass my exams.*
4B *Most children are psychic up to the age of 11 or 12.*
5A *My mum warned me that I'd end up in a mental hospital.*

3 Discussion points

This can be done in open class.

p.146 VOCABULARY
Ways of looking

As an initial way of teaching the different ways of **looking**, you could mime to the students and try and elicit the appropriate word. If no one knows, you should give the word and drill the pronunciation. Students can then quickly test each other on the vocabulary by taking it in turns to mime and then guess the word being mimed.

Answers

1 watched;   2 glanced;   3 peered;   4 look;
5 seen;   6 stared;   7 gazed

pp.146–147 LANGUAGE STUDY
Abbreviating clauses

1 Write the two sentences *I'd seen Tom's spirit. It was walking beside him.* on the blackboard and see if students can make the one sentence from them.

2 Answers

1 We felt the ground start to shake.
2 Anna noticed a strange smell coming from a cupboard.
3 Did you hear their dog barking all night?
4 We listened to their footsteps coming closer.
5 The policeman caught the thief climbing through the window.
6 The children watched the farmer milking the cows.

p.147 LISTENING

To introduce the topic, ask the class what exactly they think reincarnation is, what the significance of it is and what they think about it.

Tapescript

YOLANDA: What's that book you're reading, Juliet? You seem very engrossed in it.
JULIET: What? Oh sorry, yes, it's about reincarnation. Quite riveting.
MALCOLM: Reincarnation! Ah, you surely don't believe in all that.
JULIET: That's why I'm reading this book – I'm trying to make my mind up about it.
YOLANDA: I'm absolutely positive there's something in it.
MALCOLM: But how can we know one way or the other? I mean, there's no proof, is there?
JULIET: That's what I used to think but now I'm not so sure. There are some fascinating stories in this book, you know.
MALCOLM: Oh yeah. Like what?

JULIET: Well, first of all, if we are reincarnated, this means that we must've been someone else in a previous life, right?
YOLANDA: Right. Go on.
JULIET: You see, people investigating reincarnation came up with the idea that if you hypnotized someone, they might be able to go back in time and tell you about their previous lives. And one of ...
MALCOLM: What a load of old rubbish! Do you believe this?
YOLANDA: Come on, Malcolm. Let Juliet finish what she has to say.
JULIET: Thank you, Yolanda. Now, as I was saying, one of the people they hypnotized was someone called Jane Evans and she managed to recall something like six or seven lives. She'd been a Jewish girl who was murdered during the Middle Ages, a servant to one of Henry VIII's wives and a nun in a convent in the USA.
MALCOM: Blimey! She'd been busy. I mean, come off it! She'd probably read some stories about these characters somewhere or other. I'm sure there's a logical explanation for all of this.
JULIET: Well, maybe you're right. She could have read something which entered her subconsciousness. That's certainly true in the case of one of her other lives. She claimed to be the servant to a French merchant. And all of the details she could remember of this past life were readily available in books. Strangely enough though, she forgot to mention the fact that the merchant was married and had five kids.
MALCOLM: There you are. What did I tell you?
JULIET: Hold on a minute! Going back to the Jewish girl, what's incredible about this past life is that she could say exactly where the girl had been killed, under a church in a, in some kind of cellar. No sooner had she told this story than some archaeologists found it. Quite by chance – they were doing some other work on the church – when they came across it and they found some skeletons down there!
Malcolm: Skeletons? You'd surely expect to find skeletons under a church, or at least I would.
Yolanda: I'm afraid I agree with Malcolm, Juliet. Were there any other cases?
JULIET: Well there's another one that's very interesting. A housewife called Dolores was hypnotized and she took on the character of someone called Gretchen Gottlieb. Now she was murdered in Germany in a forest during the last century and what's interesting about this case is that, when she was hypnotized, Dolores spoke in German and yet she'd never learnt the language at school or anything. What's more, when she came out of hypnosis, she couldn't speak any German at all.
YOLANDA: What was her German like?
JULIET: Well, not very good, I'm afraid. It was pretty incorrect and she avoided using verbs. Some of her answers didn't make sense and some of the time she hadn't understood questions she'd been asked.

MALCOLM: So did this Gretchen actually exist?

JULIET: Well, they tried to verify the story but they couldn't confirm it either way. There weren't any records or anything like that.

KRISHNA: Do you think Dolores was trying to take the researchers in?

YOLANDA: Well, according to the book, they were sure she was acting in good faith but, well, you never know.

MALCOLM: In good faith! If you believe that, you'll believe anything.

Answers

1B Yolanda says she's positive there's something in it. Juliet is trying to make up her mind, Malcolm totally disbelieves it.

2B a Jewish girl, a servant to one of Henry VIII's wives, a nun and a servant to a French merchant

3D

4C

5B Some of her answers didn't make sense. The answer isn't C because it is clear that she made a lot of mistakes.

p.147 PRONUNCIATION

1 Play the relevant part of the *Listening* again and see if students hear the tone of disbelief.

2 **Tapescript and Answers**

1 His own daughter. (*surprise*)
2 His own daughter. (*disbelief*)
3 His own daughter. (*simple statement*)
4 By car. (*simple statement*)
5 By car. (*disbelief*)
6 By car. (*surprise*)

pp.147–148 LANGUAGE STUDY
no sooner and *not only*

1 Before looking at the book, you may want to isolate the target sentence on the tape and get students to take it down as dictation and then in small groups analyse the exact meaning. They can then compare their explanation with that in the book.

Answers

1 After these constructions we invert the subject and the verb/auxiliary.
2 We generally use these structures for emphasis.
3 Adverbs of frequency with 'negative force', e.g. *seldom, rarely, never* when they begin a sentence.

2 **Answers**

1 No sooner had she arrived than she started to complain.
2 Not only does he sing but he also dances.

3 I have never eaten such an awful meal.
4 When fighting broke out, the match had just started.
5 This exercise is not only tedious, it is also hard.
6 No sooner had we put up the tent than it started to rain.

p.148 VOCABULARY
Extreme adjectives

1 Answers

interesting/fascinating
beautiful/gorgeous
big/huge
hungry/starving
small/tiny
sure/positive
good/wonderful
hot/boiling
frightened/terrified
bad/awful
tired/exhausted
cold/freezing

2 Answers

1 correct; 2 wrong; 3 correct; 4 wrong; 5 correct; 6 correct

• We modify **ordinary** adjectives like *cold* with modifiers like *fairly, quite, very* and *extremely*. We modify **extreme** adjectives like *freezing* with modifiers like *absolutely, completely, utterly* and *totally*. Note that *quite* and *really* can be used with both types of adjective.

3 Answers

1 starving; 2 tiny; 3 freezing; 4 awful;
5 wonderful; 6 terrified; 7 gorgeous;
8 fascinating; 9 huge; 10 exhausted; 11 positive;
12 hungry

Extension

Students should be given five minutes to prepare to tell to another student a strange or extraordinary experience they have had incorporating the various adjectives and modifiers as appropriate. You should have one to tell first as an example.

p.149 WRITING
The mysterious hitchhiker

1 Ask half the class to read the first version and half the class to read the second. Put students in A/B pairs and they tell their version to their partner and note if there are any differences. Then all students look at both versions and analyse the differences. Note that the second version is incomplete and that it uses a greater variety of tenses, sentence length and construction than the first version. Extra details are given to make the story more interesting and the vocabulary is much richer.

2 Extension

When the students have written the end of the story, they may like to read it out to the class. As an additional fluency activity you could ask students to act out the story of the mysterious hitchhiker with their endings.

3 This could be set as homework.

pp.150–151 READING
Understanding the mysteries of intuition

1 Having decided on an order, tell the class the order that we suggest and let them discuss what they think of it. If they disagree, ask them to say why, and more importantly get them to suggest any extra stages that they would include.

Answers
5, 7, 2, 3, 6, 1, 4

2 Do this timed (10 – 15 minutes) and individually, comparing answers in open class at the end.

Answers
1A *The two ...* (i.e. mother and elder sister)
2B *Of the second dream ...* the third occasion was not a dream.
3D *I would have put it down to mere coincidence if it had not been repeated twice.*
4D *The first occasion ... when I was seven years old ... the second dream about ten years later*
5B The friend arrived later for lunch.

p.151 USE OF ENGLISH

Give students about one minute to quickly read through the text. Tell them, before they read, that afterwards they must write down what they consider to be the four or five main points of the story. When they have done this, they should compare their points with a partner to see if they agree. They should refer back to the text to discuss any major differences. Then individually or in pairs let them attempt to complete the spaces. If this is done as a timed exercise, allow 10 to 15 minutes.

Answers
1 or;   2 whose;   3 victims;   4 following;   5 used;
6 living;   7 would;   8 in;   9 the;   10 one;
11 on;   12 flower;   13 all;   14 down;   15 sooner;
16 with;   17 You;   18 dare/can/could;   19 into;
20 away

p.152 VOCABULARY

Put students in small groups to do this. When each group has finished, regroup students to compare their ideas and justify their choices. Finally, give out the answers and deal with any common problems.

Answers
1 D;   2 C;   3 D;   4 D;   5 A;   6 C;   7 B;   8 B;
9 A;   10 B;   11 A;   12 B;   13 A;   14 B;   15 C

UNIT 14

Destination USA

Possible lesson organization

L1	SPEAKING	p.153
	READING	The Melting Pot, pp.154–155
	*LANGUAGE STUDY	The gerund and the infinitive, p.156
	Homework	
	USE OF ENGLISH	Dialogue completion, p.157

L2	LANGUAGE STUDY	Saying numbers, p.157
	LISTENING	Saying numbers, p.158
	PRONUNCIATION	Saying numbers, p.158
	*VOCABULARY	British and American English, p.158
	SPEAKING	Structured communication activity, p.159
	Homework	
	VOCABULARY	Phrasal verbs p.157

L3	LISTENING	Exam practice, pp.160–161
	*USE OF ENGLISH	pp.161–162
	WRITING	The rules of the game exs 1–3, pp.162–163
	Homework	
	WRITING	ex. 4. p.162

These are the items that are most easily done by students at home if classroom time is short.

p.153 SPEAKING

1 The main aim of this activity is to generate interest in the topic of emigration and the text which follows on pp.154 – 155

The illustrations

The background has an advertisement for a passenger ship to the USA. The top left hand picture shows immigrants having their first sight of the Statue of Liberty. From their dress they look as though they have come from Eastern Europe. The picture underneath it shows three children and their belongings. The bottom pictures show a ship full of emigrants leaving home and their reception at Ellis Island where they had to undergo a medical examination.

2 Discussion points

Put students in pairs to do this and then, after they have finished, tie the discussion together by compiling a list on the blackboard of the various reasons why people might choose to emigrate and another list of what would be difficult for someone living in a new country. In multilingual classes this needs to be done at quite a general level, but in classes where students all come from the same country the discussion can get quite specific. If you are not a native of this country, students may be interested to know what you have found difficult to adapt to, if anything. It may also be interesting to find out which is the most popular country that students would choose to emigrate to and why. If there are students with relatives who have emigrated, you may like to ask them to tell the rest of the class about the experience of their relatives.

pp.154–155 READING
The melting pot

1 If you have not done so already, ask the class to consider what reasons people had for emigrating to the USA. Then tell students to study the graph before reading the text. Ask them to say what it tells them about the changing nature of immigration in the 19th century. Then get them to read *The melting pot* text. (You could ask them to write a written summary of the information contained in the graph as Paper 3 practice.)

Answers
1 35 million; 2 1845 – 48; 3 more than nine million; 4 four million

2 We can arrive at the correct answers for 1, 2 and 3 by a process of elimination.
1B not A: *Religion also encouraged millions to leave the Old World.*
not C: *... many young men fled Eastern Europe to avoid being conscripted ...*
not D: *Following the collapse of the economy ...*
2D *One major cause of the exodus among European peasants was the rise in population.*
3B not A: *... factories were calling out for labour ...*
not C: *... there was the promise of land.*
not D: *Men were needed to open up the West.*
4B *By 1890 among a total population of 63 million, there were more than 9 million foreign-born Americans.*
5D *Nor should we forget the equally awful fate of the American Indians.*

p.156 LANGUAGE STUDY
The gerund and the infinitive

1 Ask students to read through part 1 and work on exercises 2 and 3 in pairs. When they have had enough time, put all the additional verbs thought of for either group on the blackboard.

2 Answers

1 emigrating; 2 to let; 3 entering; 4 to allow; 5 to deport; 6 crossing; 7 to hide; 8 showing; 9 filling in; 10 not to understand; 11 to be

3 Answers

+ infinitive	+ gerund
refuse agree threaten offer pretend tend	consider deny avoid mind finish

4 Let students work on this in small groups and then put the groups together to compare their ideas on which ones demonstrate an important change in meaning and in what way the meaning is different.

Answers

1 no difference
2 big difference – in the first sentence *remembering* came before *closing the window*.
3 no big difference here although you would not usually use the gerund to describe a habit, e.g. You wouldn't say *I like washing my car on Sundays*.
4 big difference – the first sentence is in the passive sense, the second active.
5 big difference – similar to 2
6 quite a subtle difference – *learning Japanese* was her final goal. *Learning ten words a day* was the method she used.

5 Answers

1 to go/picking up; 2 seeing; 3 to rain*
4 playing/to play; 5 to study/studying; 6 driving;
7 to make/to concentrate; 8 to wonder; 9 to do;
10 jogging; 11 to post; 12 to do; 13 lending;
14 taking off
*(We don't use the gerund after a continuous tense)

p.157 USE OF ENGLISH

Before the students start the exercise, explain the situation and ask them to suggest likely questions.

Answers

1 When did your family come over?
2 Why did he decide to emigrate?
3 Did he come on his own?
4 Have you ever been back to Ireland?
5 What was it like?
6 Do you still keep in touch with them?

p.157 VOCABULARY
Phrasal verbs in this unit

1 Answers

1 D; 2 F; 3 E; 4 H; 5 A; 6 B; 7 C; 8 G

2 Answers

1 catching on; 2 carry them out; 3 going up;
4 talked me into; 5 settled down; 6 set up;
7 took up; 8 let you down

p.157 LANGUAGE STUDY
Saying numbers

Answers

1 She lived for *a* hundred years.
2 The population of the USA is over 200 *million*.
3 Five *thousand* people visit the gallery every day.
4 My telephone number is *two- four- double three - eight - nine - five.*
5 I would like *a dozen eggs,* please.
6 The code for London is o (*oh*) one.
7 Dozens of people walked out of the film. (*correct*)
8 The book is one hundred *and* eighty pages long. The book is one hundred eighty pages long in American English (AE)
9 Altogether that's three *pounds sixty*-five.
10 The average family has two *point* four children.
11 The drawer is an *eighth* of an inch too wide.
12 There were thousands of people at the party. (*correct*)
13 The Battle of Waterloo was in *eighteen fifteen.*
14 My car *does* thirty miles *to the gallon.*

p.158 LISTENING

Tapescript and Answers

1 *Phone numbers*
A 0223 68991
B 010 33 1 4476 1085

2 *Account numbers*
A 87640328
B 925487234

3 *Decimals*
A 3.2
B 2.54
C 0.38

4 *Fractions*
A 1/4
B 2/3
C 3/8
D 5/16

5 *Dates*
A 11/11/1918
B 14/7/1789
   7/14/1789 (in AE)
C 1/3/1963
   3/1/1963 (in AE)

6 *Amounts*
A $6.92 cents
B £10.03p

7 *Scores*
A Lendl won the tennis match 6-0, 3-6, 6,1.
B Italy beat Holland 2-0.

8 *Large numbers*
A 23, 927, 421
B 9, 867, 364
C 989, 774

p.158 PRONUNCIATION

1 The numbers are broken up into their respective groups and said accordingly.

2 Extension

As further practice of saying numbers, you may like to give the class a simple arithmetic quiz, perhaps on a *first group to answer correctly gets the point* basis, e.g.

	1/3 – 1/4		½
	2/3 x 3/4		½
What does	10,001 – 8,764	equal?	(1,267)
	91,392 ÷ 357		(256)
	987 x 241		(6,159,867)
	4.789 x 3.204		(15.343956)

p.158 VOCABULARY
British and American English

1 Start off by discussing in open class what differences students are aware of between British and American English. Try to get them to be as specific as possible. Ask them if they know any words which are different in British and American English before letting them do exercise 1.

Answers
1 H;   2 J;   3 R;   4 N;   5 O;   6 A;   7 D;   8 L;
9 F;   10 E;   11 C;   12 P;   13 I;   14 B;   15 G;
16 Q;   17 M;   18 K

2 Answers

1 Can you go to the chemist, darling? We need some nappies for the baby and a plaster for my finger.
2 Last autumn, I was driving along the motorway when I ran out of petrol. Luckily, a lorry driver stopped and gave me a lift.
3 Our flat is quite near the underground station.
4 They sent us a telegram inviting us to spend our Christmas holidays with them.
5 It's my turn to pay the bill. Pass me my handbag; I've got a £20 note in it.
6 Biscuits and sweets are bad for our teeth.
7 Nothing works round here. Not only is the lift broken but so is the tap in the bathroom.

Extension
If you want to encourage students to use the new vocabulary productively, you could ask them to make up a story in groups or round the class (one sentence each) entitled *Murder In New York City* aiming to include as many of the new items of vocabulary as possible.

p.159 SPEAKING
Structured communication activity

Find out if any of the class have been to New York, what it's like and so on. Is the stereotype image of violence and drugs anything like the reality? If you know New York, encourage the class to ask you questions about it.

After the students have worked on the activity and as a way of presenting what they have done, you can ask each group in turn to try and persuade you to join *their* group for the day because it has the most varied and interesting programme of events.

pp.160–161 LISTENING

Examination advice
Let the students read through this section quickly and then ask them to summarize in their own words a) what you **must** do and b) what you **mustn't** do during the Paper 4 exam.

For the three listening exercises we would suggest treating them very much as practice exam material and thus have the class listen straight through twice without conferring. You may even decide to give out the correct answers immediately before discussion to show exactly how the class has done. The subsequent time should be spent on going over problems and listening again to the parts of the text that caused specific problems. Note that because this is regarded as more or less pure exam practice there is no tapescript at the back of the Coursebook.

1 Tapescript

GUIDE: OK, OK everybody, In a, in a minute we'll be getting off the boat but before we do, I want to tell you a little bit about the statue. Now although it's almost certainly the most famous symbol of America and its people, it was, in fact, given to us by the people of France to commemorate the friendship between the two countries. In her right hand, as you can see, is the torch of liberty and in her left hand is a tablet which has the date July 4th, 1776 on it. That's the date of American independence, of course. OK, let's give you a few facts and figures about the statue. The idea of the statue came from a French historian and the money for it was raised by the French people. It was designed by Frederic Bartholdi, that's B-A-R-T-H-O-L-D-I. The statue was made of copper sheets which were hammered together by hand. They had to be put together over a huge framework of four supports which were made by Eiffel, the guy responsible for the Eiffel Tower in Paris, France. It was finished in 1885 and then taken to pieces to be shipped from France to the USA. And it weighs 25 tons.

   Now the statue itself is 151 feet high but, if you add the pedestal, that's what the statue stands on, then it makes 305 feet which is 93 metres. If you want to go right, if you want to go right to the top, then I'm afraid you've got to walk. There's an elevator up through the pedestal but from then on you have use a spiral staircase to reach the observation point in the lady's crown and it's 171 steps! Just to finish off, before we dock, when the statue had been reconstructed, it was dedicated by President Grover Cleveland on 28th October, 1886. OK, we're nearly there.

Answers
1 July 4th, 1776;   2 Frederic Bartholdi;   3 Copper;
4 1885;   5 151 feet;   6 305 feet;   7 93 metres;
8 25 tons;   9 28th October, 1886

2 Tapescript

ANDY: Before we go to this game, can you tell me a little bit about the rules?

GUS: Sure. What do you want to know?

ANDY: Well, I know there are 11 men on the field for each team at one time but what I really wanted to know was how you score points.

GUS: OK. First of all, you can score points in five different ways. The first is with a touchdown. When you cross your opponent's goal line, then you get six points.

ANDY: Although they don't actually touch the ball down, do they?

GUS: No, they don't.

ANDY: You have to in rugby.

GUS: Is that right? The second way is after the touchdown you can get an extra point by kicking the ball between the posts.

ANDY: That's just like rugby union except you get two points.

GUS: And the third way is a field goal – that's worth three points – which is when you kick the ball between the posts while the ball is in play, not after a touchdown.

ANDY: I've got it. And that's it?

GUS: Well, there are two other ways but they're a little complicated and unusual so I won't go into them right now.

ANDY: OK. Now what about the playing of the game? You can pass the ball forward in American football, correct? You can't do that in rugby.

GUS: Yes, but only once in each play. After that, it has to be passed backwards like in rugby.

ANDY: But I've never seen it happen in the games I've watched on TV.

GUS: No, it is a little unusual.

ANDY: Now the *plays*. What exactly are they?

GUS: A *play* is basically the bit of action between the two scrimmages. So, imagine a player gets tackled with the ball. The game stops and then restarts with a scrimmage – that's when the two teams face each other and everybody blocks and tackles. Then there's maybe a bit of action lasting anything from two to 20 seconds until the next touchdown or tackle or the ball goes out of play.

ANDY: I see. Oh, one more thing. How does the ball change hands between the teams?

GUS: It can be intercepted when it's thrown of course or taken off the other team but the basic idea of the game is to gain yardage and you have to gain ten yards in four plays. If you don't achieve that, then the other team is given the ball.

ANDY: It's all pretty complicated.

GUS: No, no, basically it's a very simple game, easy to understand. Now, when I went to England, someone took me to a cricket match. Now that's a complicated game.

ANDY: No, it's not. If you know baseball, then really it's quite easy ...

Answers
1C *a field goal – that's worth three points.*
2D *Yes, but only once in each play.*
3C *A play is basically the bit of action between the two scrimmages.*
4A *It can be intercepted when it's thrown of course or taken off the other team.*
5D *... to a cricket match. Now that's a complicated game.*

3 Tapescript

CHRISSY: You're a Mormon, aren't you Gina?

GINA: Well, yes I was brought up as a Mormon, if that's what you mean, but I don't go to church as often as I should.

CHRISSY: Is it part of the Christian Church?

GINA: Oh, yes.

CHRISSY: I'm sorry to be so ignorant but when did it all start?

GINA: You can date it from 1827.

CHRISSY: What happened then?

GINA: That's when the prophet Joseph Smith was visited by an angel called Moroni.

CHRISSY: Moroni?

GINA: Yes, and he took Smith to a place where there were some gold plates buried and these plates had a holy book enscribed on them, the Book of Mormon. Mormon was Moroni's father by the way.

CHRISSY: This sounds a bit like Moses receiving the Ten Commandments.

GINA: Exactly. The thing is, with God's help, Smith was able to read what was written on the plates, 'cause it had been written in a kind of Ancient Egyptian. And after that, the cult really caught on and lots of people joined it.

CHRISSY: And what happened to the plates?

GINA: They were destroyed.

Chrissy: I see. And how come this happened in America?

GINA: Good question. The Bible talks of lost tribes of Israel and the idea is that one of these tribes made it to America and that's how the plates came to be buried there.

CHRISSY: What's special about being a Mormon? I mean, in what ways is it different from other forms of Christianity?

GINA: First, baptism is very important. not just for the individual but also for the ancestors of the individual.

CHRISSY: The ancestors?

GINA: Yes, you can bring your ancestors into the Church when you join. And there are very strict rules on drinking. You can't, you can't drink any stimulants: coffee, tea, alcohol. And no cigarettes.

CHRISSY: Sounds a bit tough.

GINA: Maybe, but it's been shown that Mormons live longer than the average American because of their healthy life style.

CHRISSY: And what about marriage? Is it true that the men can have more than one wife?

GINA: They used to but it's not allowed any longer.

Answers

1 False – *Well, yes I was brought up as a Mormon, if that's what you mean, but I don't go to church as often as I should. She still considers herself a Mormon.*

2 True – *Is it part of the Christian Church? Oh, yes.*

3 False – *You can date it from 1827.*

4 False – *Smith was visited by Moroni ...*

5 True – *This sounds a bit like Moses receiving the Ten Commandments. Exactly.*

6 False – *... it had been written in a kind of Ancient Egyptian.*

7 True – *And after that, the cult really caught on and lots of people joined it.*

8 True – *The Bible talks of lost tribes of Israel and the idea is that one of these tribes made it to America and that's how the plates came to be buried there.*

9 True – *... you can bring your ancestors into the Church when you join.*

10 False – *Is is true that the men can have more than one wife? They used to but it's not allowed any longer.*

pp.161–162 USE OF ENGLISH

1 Answers

1 shameful; 2 independence; 3 safety; 4 opposition; 5 immigration; 6 departure; 7 championship; 8 failure; 9 friendship

2

Find out what the class knows about baseball, where it is played (apart from the USA), what equipment you use, how many players in a team and a basic idea of the rules if possible. Then let students attempt the exercise either together or individually as exam practice to time (*approx. 7 mins.*).

Answers

1 obvious/understandable; 2 take; 3 then; 4 in; 5 quiet/soft; 6 enough; 7 caused; 8 up; 9 been; 10 Since; 11 taken; 12 have; 13 even/already; 14 fewer; 15 on; 16 so; 17 biggest; 18 the; 19 when/where; 20 in

pp.162–163 WRITING
The rules of the game

1 Answers

1 outfield; 2 infield; 3 pitcher; 4 diamond; 5 foul line; 6 batter; 7 strike zone

2

1 True – *It is played on a large field which has a diamond-shaped area in one corner where the main action takes place.*

2 False – *... two teams of nine players each take it in turns to bat while the other fields.*

3 True – *... if he misses three times, he is out ...* *– If a fielder catches the ball in the air, touches the base with the ball before the runner gets there ...* *– or succeeds in touching the runner between bases while holding the ball.*

4 True – *A run is scored by the batter safely making his way all the way round the bases without being out. Doing this with one hit is called a home run.*

5 False – *... he must hit the ball into fair territory ... not behind the foul lines.*

6 True – *The pitcher isn't allowed to deliver the ball outside the strike zone.*

3 Analysis

1
Para. 1	– where the game is played
Para. 2	– the object of the game
Para. 3	– how play starts
Para. 4	– the aim of the batter and how he/she can be 'out'
Para. 5	– restrictions on the pitcher

2
- **have to**: if the batter manages to hit the ball then he *has to* drop the bat ...
- **must**: he *must* hit the ball into fair territory.
- **can**: only a single runner *can* ... the batter *can* (i.e. is allowed to) move to the next base.
- **allow**: the pitcher isn't *allowed* to deliver the ball.
- **prohibit**: it is *prohibited* to throw the ball at the batter.

3 field; infield; outfield; base; team; player; fielder; bat; batter; home run; pitcher; umpire; strike and strike zone; fair territory; foul lines

Extension

Having completed the above exercises, students could
be asked to explain the rules of baseball to a partner.
Listen out for any problems with the use of appropriate modals and correct before going on to the extension
activities.

or

Put students in pairs. Student A has to describe a well-
known game to his or her partner and see how long it
takes them to recognize what it is.

or

Describe the rules of a game to the class which they
then play, e.g. *Botticelli* – the rules are as follows:
Botticelli is a game for any number of people. The aim
of the game is to guess the identity of a person, living
or dead. The group nominates one person to begin (X);
this person thinks of somebody famous and says the
first letter of the subject's name. If the subject was
William Shakespeare, this would be 'S'.
Students then think of questions whose answers would
begin with 's' e.g. *What is the religion of Japan? (Shinto)*
If the person who is asked does not know the answer
then a direct question can be asked, e.g. *Is he dead? (Yes)*
and so on, until the person is identified.

UNIT 15

Our Common Future

Possible lesson organization

L1	SPEAKING VOCABULARY PRONUNCIATION USE OF ENGLISH *READING	pp.164–165 Work and New Technology, p.165 Word building, p.165 p.166 The menace of the micro, pp.166–167
	Homework Ask students to read through *Language study* ex. 1 on p.168 as preparation. Ask students to bring in some of their most recent compositions next lesson for *Writing* ex. 3, p.171.	

L2	LANGUAGE STUDY WRITING **Homework** LANGUAGE STUDY	More complex ways of talking about the future exs 1–3, pp.168–169 The opinion composi- tion – including timed composition, pp.170–171 ex. 4, p.169

L3	LISTENING USE OF ENGLISH READING *USE OF ENGLISH **Homework** USE OF ENGLISH	p.172 A final look, pp.172–173 In the Year 2000, p.174 ex. 1, p.175 ex. 2, p.175

*These are the items that are most easily done by students as
homework if classroom time is short.*

pp.164–165 SPEAKING
What does the future hold for us?

Prior to discussing their answers to the questionnaire
in Exercise 1 and the discussion points in Exercise 2,
you may like to help students with the range of
language for expressing opinion, agreeing and disagreeing. (See Unit 7.)

p.165 VOCABULARY
Work and New Technology

Answers
1 computer; 2 software/hardware; 3 word
processor; 4 training course; 5 skills; 6 robot;
7 redundant; 8 trade(s) union; 9 strike; 10 dole

p.165 PRONUNCIATION
Word building

This exercise looks at how words can be built and the
impact that this has on pronunciation in word stress.
1 employ
em'ploy *verb*
em'ployed *past participle*
em'ployment *noun*
em'ployable *adjective*
em'ployer *noun*
'unem'ployment *noun*
'unem'ployable *adjective*
'unem'ployed *adjective*
emplo'yee *noun*
2 compete
com'pete *verb*
com'petitive *adjective*
com'petitor *noun*
uncom'petitive *adjective*
compe'tition *noun*
3 qualify
'qualify *verb*
'qualified *adjective*
dis'qualify *verb*
qualifi'cations *noun*
un'qualified *adjective*
disqualifi'cation *noun*

p.166 USE OF ENGLISH

1 qualified; 2 unemployment; 3 competitive;
4 unemployed; 5 qualifications; 6 uncompetitive;
7 unemployable; 8 competitor; 9 employed;
10 competition

pp.166–67 READING
The menace of the micro

1 Let students compare ideas quickly in pairs before
getting open class feedback.

Answers
1 an expert on computers
2 They provide tremendous opportunities as well as
  threats to traditional forms of employment.
3 This is for the students to decide.

2 Give students time to work through the multiple
choice questions individually and then compare their
ideas in small groups, justifying their answers from
appropriate parts of the text.

Answers

1B These developments in technology are bound to have a dramatic effect on the future of work.

2A Postmen ... will vanish in a paper-free society.

3C A Even people in traditional professions ... are unlikely to escape the effects of new technology.
B Doctors too ...
D a computer judge would ... judge your case more fairly.

4D Children will still go to school ... where they can make friends and develop social skills.

5D ... People should get computer literate.

6C Whether the future is one of ... how the relationship between work and reward is viewed.

Extension

Divide the class into As and Bs, where As are the weaker students. The As should read through the text again, familiarizing themselves with the various arguments, preparing to argue them as **their own point of view.** The Bs should go through the article again but in order to prepare arguments **against** all the various points and opinions. When students have had enough preparation time, put them into A/B pairs to argue their respective cases.

pp.168–169 LANGUAGE STUDY
More complex ways of talking about the future

1 The future perfect

The explanation in part 1 can either be used as the basis for your presentation of the grammar point from the blackboard or students could be asked to read through the section as preparatory homework. In going through the answers to exercise 2, make sure that students are able to contract *will have,* i.e. *I'll've finished.*

Answers

2 A I will have finished this exercise in five minutes' time.
B By the end of the century doctors will have found a cure for AIDS.
C They will have arrived by ten o'clock this evening
D ... but they will be tired and hungry because they will not have slept or eaten.
E By next April I will have been out of work for six years.
F A super-intelligent computer will have been invented by the year 2000 ...
G ... and human labour will have been replaced by robots.
H ... but they still will not have found a way to replace cleaners.

2 The future continuous

Answers
3A; 1C; 2B

3 The future after introductory time expressions

Answers
2 A Office workers will have jobs until new technology makes them redundant.
B Factory workers will go on strike as soon as robots are/have been introduced.
C Once computers are programmed with all the information they will act as judges.
D Scientists won't have discovered an alternative source of energy before oil runs out.
E Immediately super-intelligent computers are invented, technicians will be needed to maintain them.
F After all these changes take/have taken place, our world will be transformed.

4 For fun, you might like to let students predict firstly for themselves in note form under given headings, e.g. *family, job, achievements,* and then for one or two other students. They should then get into groups with the people they have predicted for, tell them their predictions and see how much similarity they bore to the students' description of their own future. They can write the paragraph predicting their own future for homework based on their notes.

p.170 WRITING
The opinion question – a final look

1 Corrections

Among the mistakes we could expect our students to correct within the five minute time limit are:

1 ...try to reduce the number of employees who are replaced by computer (*meaning is opposite to the intended one*)
2 industry tries (*concord*)
3 'person' should be people
4 We 'use' computers, we don't 'manipulate' them (*collocation*)
5 mainly look for (*wrong phrasal verb and word order*)
6 We 'do business', we don't 'make business' (*collocation*)
7 They don't give university students the chance... (*word order*)
8 introduce themselves *(vocabulary)*
9 on the other hand (*delete, unnecessary*)
10 take an orientation *(vocabulary)*
11 technology (*spelling*)
12 self-satisfied *(vocabulary)*
13 ...don't go *(pronoun is missing)*
14 If (*not 'once' - perhaps caused by interference from L1*)
* Indicate incoorect usage for corrections

Model answer

Unemployment among young people is constantly increasing. The reason behind this is that organizations try to replace employees with computers and their operators.

The problem is that companies look for well qualified people with a lot of experience because they want them to carry out important work immediately. This means that university graduates are not given the opportunity to join firms.

Young people who are in work tend to over-specialize and have little knowledge of other areas. I think that students should have a broad training in technology, public relations and services so they are qualified for different types of work.

A further problem is that students give up too easily. If they do not immediately find the ideal job, they choose the easy option of unemployment.

2 Answers

8 to 11 – there are not too many basic mistakes.

3 While students are looking through old compositions and drawing up a 'favourite mistakes' list, you may want to go round the class and have a brief chat to each student about their particular approach to the composition paper.

4 Ask students to read this, then have a short open-class discussion with students making comments, expressing agreement/disagreement with the advice and so on.

5 To be done under exam conditions.

p.172 LISTENING

Let students attempt this more or less under exam conditions, i.e. a minute or so to look through the questions and then the tape played through twice with a short gap between each play through. At the end, let students say what problems they had, why they got things wrong and so on. Discuss ways of avoiding or getting round these problems.

Part one tapescript

INTERVIEWER: In Britain we are often told that people are leaving the big cities to live in the countryside but is this the case worldwide?

EXPERT: Not at all. If you look at the biggest cities in 1950, seven out of the top ten were in the developed countries but by the year 2000 the developing countries will have eight out of the top ten. New York, which in 1950 was number one with a population of around 12 million, will only be the sixth largest city in the world but with an extra two million.

INTERVIEWER: And London?

EXPERT: London, which was number two, won't even be in the top ten. Its population in 1950, by the way, was about ten million.

INTERVIEWER: And why is this happening? Why are people moving to the big cities from the country in developing countries?

EXPERT: The reasons are complex but many are moving to look for work. And the problems this creates are enormous. It's estimated that 26 million people will be living in Mexico City by the year 2000, with São Paulo in Brazil not far behind.

INTERVIEWER: It's difficult to believe.

EXPERT: I know. Rio De Janeiro will have a population of a mere 13 million. Well, just imagine the kinds of difficulties this is going to cause in terms of health, transport and education.

INTERVIEWER: Yes. What about the cities of Asia? Will they be experiencing a similar sort of growth?

EXPERT: In some cases, yes. Calcutta in India which was number ten in the league in 1950 is expected to be the fourth biggest city in the world with a population of 16 million – quadrupling its size in just 50 years. Bombay and Delhi too are expected to be in the top ten.

INTERVIEWER: What about Japan?

EXPERT: Ah! Well, Tokyo was number three in 1950 and that's where it'll be at the beginning of the next century, although its population will have trebled to about 18 million. Looking at the other major cities in Asia, Shanghai and Seoul will be in the top ten as well but, perhaps surprisingly, not Bejing or Hong Kong.

INTERVIEWER: Now, if we could turn our attention to home, what about the trend of people moving out of the cities ...

Answers

1 seven; two

2

1950	Position in top 10	Population
New York	1	12m
London	2	10m
Calcutta	10	4m
Tokyo	3	6m

2000		
New York	6	14m
Calcutta	4	16m
Tokyo	3	18m

3   26

Part two tapescript

INTERVIEWER: Now, if we could turn our attention to home, what about the trend of people moving out of the cities like London?

EXPERT: Ah! We should be a bit careful about saying people are moving out of London. Another way of looking at it is to say London itself is moving into the country.

INTERVIEWER: How do you mean?

EXPERT: With improved transport and better living standards, people can actually afford to spread out far more than they did before and commute into town from greater distances. People can travel to work from distances that would have been inconceivable even 20 years ago.

INTERVIEWER: All the same, isn't there a drift away from the capital?

EXPERT: Oh, certainly, but it shouldn't be exaggerated. Lots of people have got fed up with the dirt and the hassle and the higher levels of crime, and have moved to the country because it's more peaceful and less stressful. And it's true companies have moved out to escape high rents and office costs, particularly in the service industries like insurance.

INTERVIEWER: Are there any specific things which has allowed this to happen?

EXPERT: One of the things which has given people more choice in where they live is the new technology. People can communicate with each other through computer networks from anywhere in the country and so work from home in the spare bedroom.

INTERVIEWER: And how has business coped with this kind of change?

EXPERT: Well, to give you one example, a company selling office equipment took the brave step of closing down its London office and allowing its ex-employees, its sales people, to set up businesses on their own account from home but using the old company just as their supplier. What happened was that turnover increased dramatically, doubled in fact and everyone was happy. And in this case the new technology was crucial for fast and efficient ordering.

INTERVIEWER: Finally, what about the impact of this trend on agriculture? Assuming that people are moving to the country, doesn't this mean that there is less land to farm?

EXPERT: Yes, indeed. And there's no doubt that we're losing fields for housing. But this doesn't matter too much as we have in recent times been overproducing and also yields from the land have increased with modern, scientific farming methods. So what's happening is that we are getting more from less.

Answers

1 False – they can commute into town from greater distances.
2 True – ... *isn't there a drift from the capital? Oh, certainly* ...
3 True – *Oh, certainly, but it shouldn't be exaggerated.*
4 False – some insurance companies have moved out of London.
5 True – *people have got fed up with the dirt ... and have moved to the country because it's more peaceful and less stressful.*
6 False – it did not have to but *took the brave step of closing down its London office.*
7 False – it has increased its turnover.
8 True – *we're losing fields for housing.*

pp.172–173 USE OF ENGLISH
A final look

Here are three possible ways of treating the material from here to the end of the unit:
a) as pure exam practice to be done more or less under exam conditions (excluding the final composition).
b) as classwork where students work on an exercise, confer, are given the answers and then go over problems.
c) as a mixture of classwork and homework.

1 Answers

1 by; 2 homes/bases; 3 have; 4 every;
5 Once; 6 where; 7 along/down; 8 the;
9 beating; 10 would; 11 just/even; 12 had;
13 quite/completely; 14 right; 15 in;
16 herself; 17 From; 18 long; 19 suddenly;
20 all

2 Sentence transformations

Answers
1 It's ages since I've been to the cinema.
2 I'm having my car serviced on Monday.
3 The button was too high for him to reach.
4 We don't understand as much as they do.
5 Sue suggested that Ann should apply for the job.
6 The last time I saw him was three years ago.
7 In spite of the fact he's rich, he is extremely mean.
8 If I had read the book, I would have known the answer.
9 I'd rather we went to the cinema.
10 He still needs to be told/telling.
11 It was such a boring lesson that she fell asleep
12 Bob isn't used to his new contact lenses.
13 He was made to stay at home by his mother./He was forbidden to go out by his mother.
14 It doesn't have/need to be finished this evening./It isn't necessary to finish that this evening.
15 Unless you stop smoking, you will be ill.
16 If I were you, I wouldn't touch that switch.
17 The necessary arrangements have been made by Janet.
18 The customer wanted to know what time the manager would come back.
19 It is the first time I've tried/eaten/tasted this fruit.
20 I wish I hadn't broken the vase.
21 Don't let me forget to water the plants.
22 You'd better take the train.
23 We spent three hours (trying to open) opening the door.
24 Would you mind not smoking in here.

3 Answers

1 form; 2 interview; 3 training; 4 retirement;
5 Unemployment

4 Answers

1 looked into; 2 look up; 3 look the engine over;
 4 looking forward to; 5 look down on

p.174 READING
In the Year 2000

Answers

1 B
2 D *A clean healthy environment*
3 C *We are tomorrow's generation. We will make it
       whatever it is.*
4 B *Somehow the world's money would have to be divided
       out ...*
5 A *I would help them to grow crops.*

p.175 USE OF ENGLISH
Reading and processing information

Model answers

> *Anna Lindsop seems to be most worried about* the
> threat of nuclear war. She thinks the world could
> be a better place if all the money spent on weapons
> was spent on helping the Third World. She would
> also like to see more religious tolerance.
> *Graham Gomez seems to think the way to solve the
> world's problems is by* dividing up money more
> fairly so everyone in the world has enough to live
> a decent life.
> *Samantha Corrigan seems afraid of* the way countries
> can build atomic bombs so easily. Social problems
> such as crime and unemployment worry her
> deeply.
> *Anthony Twist imagines a world where everybody* will
> live in peace and fight to create a healthy environ-
> ment by reducing noise and pollution and increas-
> ing civic amenities. However, his greatest concern
> is that people nowadays are too selfish and violent
> and he would like to see them become kinder.
>
> © Copyright Longman Group UK Ltd. 1989